Bonded at Birth:

An Adoptee's Search for Her Roots

Gloria Oren

Let thy father
and thy mother
be glad,
And let her
that bore thee
rejoice.

This book received a special blessing from my birth father's second wife, Mrs. Jennifer Longley. The text is from Proverbs 23:25 (known as the book of Mishlay in Hebrew).

This book is the product of the author's personal experiences and her observations. All of the stories are true and are based on actual happenings in which some of the individuals mentioned were given fictitious names to protect their privacy. Any similarity to scenarios or wording found elsewhere is purely coincidental.

ISBN: 978-0-692-72228-2
Library of Congress Control Number: 2016908907

First printing June, 2016

PRINTED IN THE UNITED STATES OF AMERICA

Dedication

I dedicate this book to the following people:

To my wonderful mother and father, Zindel and Anya Oxenhorn, AKA Sidney and Hannah, who adopted me as an infant. Unfortunately, they could not see it published, nor share in my happiness of contacting my birth family. And to my biological mother Marcia (Fritz) McCabe.

To my biological maternal grandmother, Aida Fritz, who played a crucial role in my adoption placement. If not for her concern and devotion, I don't know where I would have ended up. May you rest in peace knowing Mom and I are together.

To my husband, Tuvia, and our three children, Chanan, Shai, and Galit who stood by me throughout my search efforts and the years of preparation of this book. Thanks to my children, I have been able to experience motherhood and gain insight into feelings and bonding involved in being a mother.

Last, I dedicate this book to the many helpful and supportive members of the Adoptees Internet Mailing List who were always there for me when I needed a shoulder to lean on. Unfortunately, this list no longer exists. I'm sure there are others like it online you can join, and I do encourage you to seek them out.

Acknowledgements

I wish to thank a few specific people who have helped me put together this memoir.

First, Jay Freeman, my cousin, for providing me with the facts I had not known or been aware of for so many years, which he had mentioned in his book *From Brooklyn I Saw Mountains.*

Second, Elisa Sananman, Jay's sister, who supported me in my search and provided more helpful information.

Third, my work in progress readers: Alpha Muser Critique Group members (Susan Dawson-Cook, Jill Earl, Michele Graf, Katie Hines, Sandra Kenny, Angie Mangino, Mary Nickum, Bob Ruehrdanz, Amber Starfire, and Fiona Young-Brown); Peg Lauber, Jennifer Longley, and Marcia McCabe, who carefully critiqued my book and advised me on ways to improve my original first draft.

Fourth, Michele Graf for editing and leading me through the early editorial stage making my memoir far better than it was at the start and to Charlene Marion for adding her insight to those editorial comments.

Fifth, my beta readers Robin Tidwell, Barbara Gini, Eugene Goodheart, Jay Freeman, Elisa Sananman, and Carol Woien.

Sixth, to Yehudah Miklaf, the husband of my biological mother's cousin, who with the help of friends located me and contacted me through my father-in-law in Israel. If not for this, we would still search for each other today.

Seventh, to Debbie Wilson for the layout design and the cover design.

And finally, yet most important, I wish to thank my fellow genealogy researchers and family members working on the Longley family, my paternal birth family, and associated families for the information many of them have made available from various sources on the Internet or through email. If it would only be as easy to research Eastern European ancestors, my other family research would grow, too.

Table of Contents

Introduction

I feel the need to share the story of my adoption because it grew into something unique.

In the adoption of a newborn, an original birth certificate identifies the name of the mother birthing the child along with the child's biological father. After the finalization of the adoption, an amended birth certificate is prepared with the adoptive parents names including the child's new name. The authorities place the original birth certificate in the sealed records. The adoptive parents receive a copy of the amended one.

Mine was different. My parents received a document thought to be an amended certificate. The document wasn't. It seems that it was a common practice in the 1950s for the attending obstetrician to provide a doctored original birth certificate with the adoptive parents' names listed as the birth parents with the baby's adopted name. This was what my birth certificate turned out to be. My birth mother didn't have the choice of naming me before transferring parental rights through adoption. I wasn't the only one. Medical staff members did the same action to the birth certificates of many other adoptees. It is interesting to note I met with a challenge when looking further into this, but am not one to give up when challenged. There is still hope to one-day get to the root of what happened then, and discover what led the medical staff members to act in such a manner.

I hope that by telling my story it will encourage other adoptees to begin a search for their biological parents. At the least, they will gain satisfaction knowing their origins and possibly their medical history.

To get a better grasp, you need to understand the basics. Five different types of adoption exist, each with its own method of operation: private adoption, agency adoption, government adoption (through the Child Protective Services), international adoption, and more recently, open adoption (since the 1970s).

Aside from the open adoption environment, all other types of adoption are closed. This means that government officials sealed the adoption records, along with medical history records and original birth certificates, making them inaccessible to the adoptee, even after the age of eighteen.

The following states have opened adoption records to the adult adoptee. They are Alabama (August 1, 2000), Alaska, Colorado (Jan 2016), Delaware, Illinois, Indiana (Feb 2016), Kansas, Maine, New Hampshire, New Jersey (Jan 2016), Ohio, Oregon, Rhode Island (July 2012), Tennessee (September 27, 1999), and Washington. Others that are partially open include: Iowa (before 07/01/1941), Maryland (before 06/01/1947), Massachusetts (before 04/14/1974), Michigan (if birth parent's rights were terminated before 05/28/1945 or on/after 09/12/1980), Minnesota (after 08/1/1982), Connecticut (finalized after 10/01/1983), Montana (if birth occurred, at least, thirty years ago), and Vermont (finalized after 07/01/1986), New York is still under debate. All six Canadian provinces have or will have open records.

I had no starting point for my search except the basic identity questions I wondered about. Who was I? Where did I come from? Did I have roots? How did I fit into this world? And later on, had I bloomed, and could I help others bloom, too?

As a young child whom my parents adopted, I didn't understand the enveloped environment of secrecy and the lies that blanketed the facts of adoption in my family. Were my mother and father trying to protect me? If so, from what would they protect me? Was it the lack of confidence holding them back from discussing the issue? Or was it the fear I wouldn't love them? My parents never discussed adoption, mine or in general.

The increase, since the 1970s, in open adoptions, permits biological parents to support contact with the son or daughter adopted as a child and the party to the adoption. So, the umbrella of secrecy, which shielded my life, seldom exists in cases of open adoption today.

Children, growing up in their biological family environment, either know or have access to their original birth certificates. They are aware of their names given at birth, their biological, ethnic, and religious backgrounds. They either know or have access to their medical and social history. More important, the biological infant bonds with its biological parents, under normal circumstances.

I, as an adoptee, lacked all of the above-mentioned basics in life. Most parents form a tight bond with the child whom they adopt, as mine did, but it's a different connection. Separated from my birth mother a few days after birth, I felt the loss internally, the black hole of the unknown, call it what you may, since learning at four that I was adopted. Some people may argue that this could be a valid reason not to tell the adopted child the facts of his or her origin. I disagree; how could I, as a child under four, know what the black hole felt like if I had everything I needed and parents who loved me? After finding out about my adoption in an unusual manner, I learned to understand the feelings, as I grew older. I believe the warning to keep my adoption a secret fueled those feelings. I also believe it's an integral part of the adoptee's self, sometimes buried, and undisclosed, but there. These basic rights, to have free access to my personal records, birthright, and culture, weren't available. Secrecy and sealed adoption records were part of the burden of being adopted that left me clueless about my biological legacy and cultural heritage.

The pain after learning things I always considered true but weren't, was worse than hearing the truth. Not only did they keep my adoption a secret, but my mother and father lied about their first child, my non-biological brother's status. They told me he was their biological son when they had adopted him, too. The facts may have been painful to process, but the secrecy and lies only made it harder. Could my adoptive parents not see this? Since both of my parents passed away years ago, this question remains unanswered. Had a very unexpected and awkward turn of event not taken place, I doubt my parents would have ever told me I was adopted. In fact, even when that event took place mommy remained hesitant about my adoption. Daddy never said a word to the day he died.

When I was old enough to understand what being an

adoptee meant, I believed I had the right to know where I came from, who my ancestors were, and what my medical history had in store for my future family and me. I would never know unless I could find my birth family. It wasn't until much later in my quest I realized I also had responsibilities toward my adoptive parents, helping them understand my need to know my history. My parents spared me from this; however, because by the time my search preoccupied me, I had become an orphan at twenty-three. As an adoptee, I learned through reading many search guides, I bore the responsibility for the way I contacted a newly found biological parent. And to be careful not to invade his or her privacy and to make sure I leave a door open for future contact if all of the parties agreed.

Even though knowledge of my adoption came at four, I still feared my adoptive parents—though I can't put my finger on the exact reason—after they repeatedly warned me to keep my adoption a secret. They were mysterious. My medical records remained incorrect, loaded with information provided using my adoptive family's history. Only after reuniting and discovering the correct information was I able to update my medical records, a task I wouldn't wish on anyone. Hard and time-consuming as it was, it was a necessary step to take for my sake and for the sake of my children.

My search turned out to be international with an American-born biological mother, who was living in Canada at the time of our meeting and a Canadian-born birth father of British ancestry. Most of his closest relatives live in Canada; a few close relatives and several distant relatives live in the United States.

Along the way, on my journey to reconnect, I made incredible discoveries related to my heritage. Who would have thought that I, an adult adoptee of a Brooklyn, New York Jewish couple, the unplanned daughter of a frightened young Jewish girl from Nova Scotia, Canada, would be related to a famous Colonel of the Revolutionary War (think the Battle of Bunker Hill), and the first North American nun? Learning this about my past meant I had roots deeper than I could have ever imagined; it meant I had a deeper cultural heritage lurking in silence within me.

With determined persistence plus the fact that both my birth mother and I were searching for each other at some point, we were successful. For me, my search was a journey that lasted sixteen years. Sixteen years of saying I would never locate my birth mother. Well, that reunion occurred and seven years later, the puzzle of my life was a full circle.

Author's Note

Bonded at Birth: an Adoptee's Search for Her Roots is a true story in which some of the individuals mentioned were given fictitious names to protect their privacy.

Throughout this book, I have referred to the Lord as G-d according to the Jewish custom of not using the fully written name in vain.

1
Before My Time

My mother-and father-to-be, Zindel and Anya Oxenhorn, welcomed my birth mother, a pregnant teenager, to their home in March 1955, to await the birth of her child.

They were Jewish immigrants from Eastern Europe, more precisely from Beltci, Bessarabia (now Moldova), sixty-eight and a half miles northwest of Chisinau, and a steppe landscape with rolling hills. The city, surrounded by wetlands, created from a waterfall landing below in the river. It was a city of short, mild winters, and long, warm summers. When Zindel was born in 1900, Beltci still looked similar to an extended village, a place that often underwent a change in control of the territory between Russia and Romania. So, my parents spoke Russian and Romanian, and Yiddish.

My adoptive father, Zindel Oxenhorn

Zindel, a good-looking man of average height, once bore a head full of hair, but by the time I was born, he was bald at the crown. His hair hugged his head around the back to the front, ending in a C-shape sideburn in front of the ears. Zindel had a love affair with suits, and the only time I can recall him not wearing a suit was when he worked the grounds or made repairs on our summer home. Zindel owned a retail business in Brooklyn. It was an outlet store, but not the outlet stores we have today, it was more characteristic of a liquidation store with various amounts of items that were available at the time, but more on that later.

Anya, a charming, appealing woman, somewhat on the heavy side with hair just short of shoulder length, stood a few inches shorter than Zindel. She tended to the home and later to their children. Just as Zindel loved suits, dresses were Anya's favorite clothing. Anya had shorts, of course, which she'd wear only in Carmel, and I can't recall her wearing pants, at least not often.

My adoptive mother, Anya Oxenhorn

They were such outgoing, friendly people that many sought their friendship. Zindel and Anya, a content couple who had been in the United States since the early 1920s, were active in their social group and in the Organization of Beltci immigrants. Yet something didn't seem right; something was missing. I will never know whether they couldn't have children of their own or chose not to take any chances of risking genetic diseases since they were first cousins. My family didn't discuss such topics. But what I know, for sure, is that they had love-filled hearts to share with both of their children whom they adopted, first a son, and then me.

Zindel and Anya told me stories and showed me filmstrips of their son, Emmanuel when I was a child. Emmanuel became ill with leukemia and passed away on October 2, 1950, just two months shy of his fourth birthday. I came to love Emmanuel as my brother though I never met him. Emmanuel, a handsome little boy, wearing a short neatly cut hairdo, and a smile that stretched from ear-to-ear, looked more intelligent than his age. I still love to view old movie strips and photos of Emmanuel from time to time.

My parents never told me that Emmanuel wasn't their biological son. I learned this from a cousin, Jay Freeman who published a book, *From Brooklyn I Saw Mountains.* When I was forty-three years old and read it, I was shocked to learn that I shared something in common with him—my parents had adopted Emmanuel. I realized then that his cancer had no connection to our parents' lineage; more exactly, it was an unfortunate, unexpected, and unforeseen turn of events.

My parents found the topic too painful to discuss. So I approached other relatives, attempting to resolve my curiosity. I didn't get very far with that either. No one mentioned that Emmanuel was adopted. Emmanuel's death, I was told, brought much grief to Zindel and Anya. The loss of a child, whether biological or adopted, is not what parents expect to happen. But G-d watched over them and had plans to heal their grief, even though it took more than five years for that ever-changing phone call to come their way when least expected.

Well-meaning friends and relatives, observing Zindel and Anya's depression, pleaded with them to take a trip for a change of scenery. In time, they decided to travel to Israel for a few weeks. The trip proved to be good therapy. It took their minds off the experienced grief and allowed them to visit with friends and relatives they hadn't seen in many years. But upon their return home, nothing had changed; their home remained childless.

Emmanuel Oxenhorn, the brother I never knew

Emmanuel's being a son who was adopted as a child might explain why his birth certificate shows his place of birth as New Jersey while Zindel and Anya lived in Brooklyn, New York. Being so young and ill, I don't believe that Emmanuel knew they adopted him. One day, as a sister of an unknown brother, I wrote a poem, in his memory:

Emmanuel

Emmanuel, as a sister you've never known

I grieve for you

Even though you were gone before, I was born.

I grieve for your birth parents,
Who probably will never know the fate
Of the child, they brought into this world.
How I wish I could find them
And tell them as much as I can
about you.
Emmanuel, little angel,
May you rest in peace
Knowing you were loved by all.
Your sister, Gloria

Around the middle of March 1955, things were bound to turn around for the Oxenhorn family. My birth mother was in her sixth month of pregnancy. She was the daughter of one of the few Jewish families living in Nova Scotia, Canada having moved there from New York. The 1950s being a time laden with paradoxes and a time of conformity versus rebellion, a time when she was in need of a solution. Research has shown that the teen birth mother of the 1950s was overwhelmed with shame and stigma associated with having a child out of wedlock. Her mother, Aida [Ross] Fritz, my maternal grandmother made connections with friends back in New Jersey, to help in this matter. These friends knew a Rabbi in New Jersey who knew another Rabbi in Connecticut. Rabbi Aaron Twersky, who just happened to be a friend of Zindel and Anya.

Rabbi Twersky called Zindel and Anya to tell them the

news of an opportunity to adopt a baby. But it was March, and the baby's due date was in June. The solution required a quick decision, though, because the birth was just weeks away. This sounded equivalent to the best news to come their way over the last five years since Emmanuel's death, but it wasn't as easy as it suggested. My birth mother was only seventeen and had to live with the family, who intended to adopt her child, until her baby was born. This, of course, is easier to talk about than to put into practice. Her family wanted no one who knew her to find out she was pregnant and had to let go of her child with no further contact. Though this meant taking in a stranger for the next three months, Zindel and Anya agreed to it. My coming into their lives helped heal their grief of having lost a son.

2
First Memories

Only one thing differentiated between most of the other babies and me born that bright, sunny spring morning of June 12, 1955, in Brooklyn, New York. My birth mother held me only once. Whether the hospital registered her under her own name, or under the name of my mother, who was going to adopt me, will stay unknown, but the hospital staff addressed her by the name Hannah. But the parent names on my birth certificate were my adoptive mother and father's names, Zindel and Anya Oxenhorn who took me home and thus into their family through adoption. My biological grandmother came to take my young birth mother, who had just gone through a traumatic experience, home to Nova Scotia.

My adoptive parents named me. Since my mother became suspicious after their adopted son, Emmanuel died of the same disease her brother Emmanuel died of, she didn't want to name me after any relative per Jewish custom. So she gave me a non-Jewish name, Gloria. I've somewhat always wondered where my name's origins came from, and at last just learned this from Elisa. I had given a copy of the manuscript to Elisa and a few other readers. When she presented her feedback we discussed several things, one of which was how I got my nickname, which I will get to later on in my story, but, for now, she provided this piece of information on how I ended up with a name that had a Latin origin.

Mommy and me near the apartment building we lived in.

The home was an apartment in a typical six-story brick faced brownstone building at 1730 Carroll Street, built circa 1930, in the Crown Heights section of Brooklyn. Crown Heights was a middle-class neighborhood with a mix of private homes and apartment buildings.

I can still picture that building clearly. The entrance sported a huge, glass French door, which leads into a small hallway. Another French door led into a large lobby. My friend Lily and her family lived in one of the two apartments on the left, and sometimes we'd ride our tricycles in circles around the lobby floor. Lily's kitchen window faced a courtyard, surrounded by six floors of apartment windows. We could access a similar courtyard by climbing through a window. It became a place where my friends and I played (hopscotch, roller-skated, or jumped rope) safely while being observed by our parents.

From the lobby, three marble stairs rose to a landing where, on the wall to the right, were the mailboxes. A long, narrow hallway lined with apartments stretched beyond the mailboxes leading to another marble staircase, the one we used. Our apartment was on the second floor, to the left of the staircase at the end of the hallway. My first bed was an empty dresser drawer lined with a pillow. This apartment is where my birth mother spent the most difficult three months of her life, awaiting my birth. This is also, where I spent my first twelve years. Later we moved to the Midwood section of Flatbush.

My adoptive parents owned an outlet store fifteen to twenty minutes from where we lived, half a block from the main drag on Pitkin Avenue in the Brownsville section of Brooklyn.

As a child, I spent much time in this store since no one was home to care for me. As I grew, I helped with the various tasks, too. I started with dusting the displays, moved on to making sure the shelves looked nice, helped set up cribs, tricycles, and strollers, and finally putting together doll carriages and strollers by myself. When I was old enough I was allowed to handle the cash register when needed. When Christmas season came around and people placed large orders on layaway I helped

Sidney's Outlet Store, the store my parents owned

pack the merchandise into boxes, a skill that has served me well later in life. In those days, people didn't consider this child labor; it was just helping and learning while doing. It would benefit children greatly if business-owning parents today would do the same.

I remember in particular our family summers. Mommy and I escaped the blazing, hot city and spent the summers in Carmel, New York where my parents owned a summer home. We cherished the cool mountain air from nearby Bear Mountain and our first breath inhaled on exiting the car made us feel refreshed. Daddy appreciated being able to escape the city and came up for weekends, at least, which meant that

Our house in Carmel, New York

during the week he had to put up with a muggy heat that made his clothes stick to his body.

Summer days in the country were usually warm and pleasant. Evenings, once the warm radiant sun set, were cool and perfect for a short stroll down the road to the reservoir. I loved the house in Carmel, the town, and the country environment. I spent my first ten summers there. In my eleventh year, we only got to Carmel on weekends, and in the following years, on rare occasions.

Every Thursday in Carmel, mommy rose early to cook and bake in preparation for Shabbat and the weekend. The aroma of homemade sweet-and-sour borscht, roast chicken, and the various puff pastries—stuffed with anything from slightly salted farmer cheese and scallions, to sweet pumpkin or salt-and-peppered mashed potatoes with fried onions, each meticulously formed in a different shape—made my mouth water.

As mommy worked, I hung around the kitchen watching her, hoping for tastes and treats. Sometimes I helped roll out the dough, cut circles in the dough with an upside down glass, or spoon the fillings onto the pastry dough. The Carmel kitchen was square-shaped, airy and lit up by two windows and a screen door. We turned on the lighting fixture when needed, which was a rare occurrence. On the other hand, the kitchen in the apartment was a narrow, rectangular room. The one window didn't allow in much light so frequent use of the lighting fixture became a necessity. Since the table sat horizontally against the window wall at the end of the room, Mommy didn't do much baking there.

"I want a pumpkin one," I begged mommy.

"Not yet. You can have one later when it's done."

Every few minutes I asked, "Is it done yet?" and Mommy replied, "Not yet."

Each Friday evening, with the preparations finished, we waited for daddy's arrival. As his car swung into the parking spot, I raced to the door, and mommy followed.

"Daddy, Daddy," I jumped off the chair running to the door.

Daddy came to the door and handed mommy the fresh challah with a soft browned crust and squishy inside, a delicacy he brought from the bakery in the city. He lifted me up, gently squeezing me in the biggest hug in the world. He put me down and hugged mommy. We were glad to see daddy, and over a late dinner, my parents shared the events of the past week. Then Sunday came, along with sadness, when daddy left to go back to the city.

Many times daddy surprised us by bringing guests, for the weekend or for a week, or two. When I was two, my cousin Elisa was fourteen. She came to visit us in Carmel. Mommy

Bath time in Carmel, New York – me and my cousin Elisa (Freeman) Sananman

filled a white aluminum bathtub outside for me to cool off in when it was hot. After playing awhile, I got my bath for the day, and Elisa combed my hair. The love Elisa and I shared then, and which continues now, was mutual.

Mention Coney Island to anyone who grew up in the late 1950s-early 1960s in Brooklyn and you'll most likely hear a response like, "Ah, Coney Island." My first trip there was at the age of three. It was a special place both young and old loved visiting. Walking along the boardwalk on a warm, late spring evening with my parents, I smelled the ocean's salty waters, blanketed by darkness, carried in the breeze. The sound of the rushing waves at night was comforting.

At some point along the boardwalk stood the grand merry-go-round and the coin-operated rides, where I waited in line with many other children for my turn. The merry-go-round wasn't the kind of gorgeous, colorful, glittering horses. Plain brown horses with various color collars and dark brown plastic molded saddles glided up and down a pole as the circular platform spun around. A black strap around the horse's neck extended far enough to secure a child in place for a safe ride. I never missed my merry-go-round ride there; that is until I outgrew it.

Another memorable feature of Coney Island was the amateur musicians lining the boardwalk. One of them was especially worth remembering. An elderly Jewish man from Russia played his violin, viola, balalaika, and mandolin. Music

In Coney Island on the merry-go-round with Mommy

filled the air, and the crowd grew bigger and bigger. Some tunes were lively and robust, others melancholic reminders of the past left behind in the old country. Tunes such as Two Guitars, Dark Eyes, and Beltz My Dear Town of Beltz filled the air from every corner. It was free ethnic entertainment at its best, enjoyable for young and old, and a great way to spend an evening. It also instilled in me a love for that music, which even today brings back memories of those nights on the boardwalk. Most were happy memories. Good quality family time together. The connection to a heritage I belonged to yet didn't or did I? The music, with lovely melodies and beats, lives on bringing comfort and peacefulness to me when needed.

Coney Island's boardwalk had other thrills too, such as the culinary experience. The biggest attraction in this nourishing jungle was no doubt Nathan's famous hot dog stand. Today's fast food is no comparison to the steam rising from those hot, succulent treats rotating on the rotisserie, juicy liquid dripping and making a crackling sound. The lines of people waiting to get their hands on one of them sometimes stretched several blocks. Besides Nathan's, interspersed along the boardwalk were vendors selling fresh buttery popcorn; sweet, luscious steaming corn-on-the-cob, and fresh spun cotton candy. No matter what you chose to consume, whether salty, sweet, buttery or bland, the Coney Island culinary experience would haunt you for the rest of your life. No wonder I loved going there. It was a magical world.

Another favorite place we visited every year was Lakewood, New Jersey. For some odd reason I always thought we visited the Catskills, but then, when visiting the area while writing this book, it dawned on me it couldn't be the Catskills since we crossed a bridge into New Jersey. But, what does a two-year-old know of geography? At that age, when you decide it's the Catskills—it's the Catskills.

My parents belonged to the Beltzer Organization, a meeting place for anyone who was originally from Beltci, Bessarabia.

In fact, daddy was once President of the organization. Once a year the organization arranged an outing to a hotel in Lakewood for members to spend the weekend together, and many times, it happened to fall on my birthday. The little kids, only a handful of us, were the center of attention. We always looked forward to this weekend. From later surfing through public domain images online of Lakewood, New Jersey hotels, I found two possibilities that were most likely one of the hotels where we stayed. It was either the Hotel Claridge or the Lexington.

On the boardwalk in Lakewood, New Jersey with Mommy and my "Goody" the cat book

Near the hotel were a boardwalk and a lake. Mommy and I took many walks there. Unlike most toddlers, my security blanket was a book called Goody: A Mother Cat Story, published by Golden Books in 1952. Goody is a story about an adventurous cat that hid her kittens from the family's children until she was ready to show them off. Everywhere I went, "Goody" the cat came, too. (Years later my daughter found the book, either on Amazon.com or in a used bookstore, and bought it for me. When I feel down, reading my Goody book helps me feel better. I look forward to sharing it with my grandchildren when the time comes.)

Life as I knew it was about to change forever when the first turning point occurred at the age of four. It's amazing to think such ordinary objects could lead to something so big—a lifetime revelation I'd carry with me wherever I'd go.

3
SHHH! It's a Secret!

My fourth birthday in Lakewood

The 1959 outing to Lakewood, New Jersey coincided with my fourth birthday. Mommy dressed me in a colorful, cute dress for dinner.

"Why am I getting dressed up?" I asked.

"You'll see. It's a surprise," she said.

"I like surprises. Let's go eat." I got excited.

Before dessert, the Beltzer members stood up singing "Happy Birthday". The waiter entered the room with a huge birthday cake.

"Where's the birthday girl?" the waiter asked, wheeling in the cake cart.

"It's me!"

"How old is the birthday girl?"

"I'm four. I'm a big girl now."

"You sure are. Let's see if you can blow out all the candles."

I took a deep breath and blew hard. All the candles went out. Everyone clapped hands; the waiter served the cake.

This was a nice start to my fifth year of life; one that would bring life-altering changes I could not have envisioned.

I lit the Shabbat candles with mommy. It is customary in many Jewish homes for mothers to train their daughters, from the age of three or four, to light the Shabbat candles so they are ready to do it on their own by the age of twelve, the year of their Bat Mitzvah. The value of lighting the Shabbat candles is to bring peace and tranquility into the home to remind us of the spiritual dimensions of Shabbat. Every Friday evening mommy would call out to me, "It's time to light Shabbat candles." Mommy lit the candles. We'd both circle them with our hands three times; then we'd cover our eyes. Mommy said the blessing, and I repeated after her. When we finished we said "Shabbat Shalom." Daddy would reply with the same. My small hands didn't cover my eyes like mommy's did, and there always seemed to be a peeking hole formed in the middle. Seeing those candles through this hole was a beautiful sight. This vision stuck with me, and many years later, it seemed as if I was seeing the light at the end of a tunnel. At that point, I did not understand how much this vision would play into my life in the years to come.

On Friday nights, our apartment building filled with the aromas of festive dinners that made us hungry. Unlike the Friday night dinner preparations in Carmel, at home in the city I didn't get to help at all. But, I cared little about that, as

Friday dinners, in the city, were a treat for me; this meant I got to eat dinner with mommy and daddy. Mommy always set the table with a challah and a filled wine cup awaiting the Kiddush (a special prayer over the wine before the Shabbat or holiday meals, followed by a blessing over the bread). First, mommy served bowls of steaming homemade chicken soup with matzo balls, noodles, or soup croutons. Next, an appetizer of some sort—a fish dish, stuffed cabbage in sweet-and-sour tomato sauce, or a vegetable salad. Then an entrée of roast chicken or stewed beef, mashed potatoes, or kasha (buckwheat) with bowtie pasta, and a vegetable pudding or steamed vegetables on the side. The meal ended with a dessert of fruit compote (a mixture of cooled, cooked fruit) and fresh baked goods.

That summer in Carmel, I helped mommy weed the rock gardens, plant and water flowers and cut the weeds pushing through the walkway. When daddy came for the weekend, I helped him trim the hedges, paint and fix things. Once when Daddy worked outside before I woke up I went out after breakfast and asked, "Can I help?"

"Sure. Pick up the pieces I cut off and make a pile."

"Okay," I said and created nice heaps of hedge trimmings. "What's that?" I asked pointing to the mountain to the east.

"That's Bear Mountain."

"Do bears live there?"

"No, silly! Bears don't live there. There's a zoo, though, with many animals. There is a large park, and a swimming pool which becomes an ice-rink in winter, and a lake with paddle boats on it," he said.

"Can we go there?" I asked.

"Maybe, one day, but right now we have work to do."

"Why do you cut the hedges?"

"To help them grow better. They need water and the sunshine to keep green. If I didn't cut them every summer, they'd overgrow and block the sun from the roots. It would be hard to water them. One day they'd block the road, too. So let's get to work. There's much to be done."

"Daddy, why can't you stay here in the summer?"

"If I stay here we wouldn't have money for food. I wouldn't be able to buy you nice clothes and the toys you like to play with. Daddy needs to work so he can do that, but I love coming out here on weekends and doing things with my precious little girl."

"Daddy, I love you, and I love helping you," I said trailing off to pick up more trimmings.

Everything was going well. That fall I started nursery school and made new friends. I loved going to school and learning things like colors, shapes, numbers, and letters. Then I had to have a tonsillectomy. Later on, my firstborn suffered from recurrent strep throat infections. By then it was no longer common to do tonsillectomies if the doctor could avoid it. Funny thing is I don't remember eating lots of ice cream; I'm sure I did. Guess it wasn't as important to me as what mommy told me after I recovered, "The doctor said you fought the anesthesia and, as a result, went through the whole procedure with open eyes although you were completely asleep."

Going through surgery, asleep yet with open eyes haunted me for many, many years. It played a major part in the anxiety I experienced later when I faced my first major surgery. There was no real reason to fear open eyes, asleep under anesthesia anyway, but fear I did to the extent that my body shook just thinking about it. When I brought it to the attention of my surgeon, he shrugged it off as nonsense, claiming never to have heard of something like that happening. But why then would mommy say such a thing? Why would she want to frighten me? He tried to reassure me everything would be okay. It was, and I came through just fine.

Life continued as usual until one specific significant day I will never forget. It was a major turning point between a stable, normal childhood (even one with older parents), which I assumed mine was, to one laden with questions, confusion, and a sense of being different.

Joseph Goldstein, in his book *Beyond the Best Interest of the Child,* wrote that many adoptees learn of their adoption in an unexpected manner, and so it was in my case.

I noticed a piece of white paper sticking out of our mailbox while playing downstairs in the lobby with my friends. I pulled it out and opened it. Someone wrote something on it, but unable to read yet I called out "Be right back," and ran upstairs to mommy. I banged on the door jumping up and down calling, "Mommy, Mommy, open. I found something."

Mommy rushed to the door and let me in. She took the note from my hand.

"Mommy, read it! What does it say?"

She stood there. Silent. From her facial expression, I was unsure what to make of it or to expect. My stomach must have felt as if tons of fluttering butterflies invaded it. Nervous and scared, I still wanted to know what the note said. "Mommy, Mommy what is it? What does it say?" I persisted.

Mommy didn't want to tell me. But, she had to decide quickly whether to make up a story or to tell me before someone else did. She seemed afraid of something, which made me even more anxious. She took a deep breath and decided, to be honest.

"Let's go sit down, and I'll tell you," she said, taking my hand and leading me to the couch.

We sat down on the arc-shaped, dark green upholstered couch in the living room, and mommy began "The note says, 'You're an adopted brat'," and then paused, perhaps waiting to see my reaction.

I turned to her with a puzzled, confused look on my face. I didn't understand what either adopted or brat meant, but she continued.

"Though you were adopted, you were and are very much loved. You're by all means not a brat," Mommy paused.

"What's adopted? What's a brat?" I asked.

Holding my hand and staring straight into space, trying to avoid this conversation, mommy continued hesitantly. "Adopted is when a baby is born to another woman, not your mommy. Your birth mother gave you to mommy and daddy as a gift to raise and to cherish you as if you were born to me. A brat is an ill-mannered, spoiled child."

"Who was the lady I was born to?" I asked.

Turning to me, with a serious look, mommy went on, "Your birth mother was a teenager. After you were born, she left the hospital to return home with her mother. Daddy and I took you home, and you became our daughter."

I knew mommy was serious and perhaps frightened, she added one last thing, "Don't tell anyone about this. You must keep your adoption a secret. No one is to know you were adopted. Do you understand? You're not to say a word about it."

Confused I asked, "Why is it a secret?"

"Because…and I don't want you to tell anybody about it. A secret is not meant to be shared."

That was it. All the information mommy ever gave me about my adoption—those few simple sentences. Confused, I wondered what was so terrible that mommy knew and didn't want me to know. This was the only time we discussed my adoption. I never dared to ask anything else then or later (well, except for one more attempt when I was eighteen, which went no better), though the questions nagged at me as I grew up. I was afraid. It was a secret, after all, and had to stay that way.

I went back to playing with my friends. They asked what the piece of paper was all about and where I'd gone.

"Somebody left a note saying they'd come to visit later. While I was upstairs mommy gave me some milk and cookies so it took a while," was my reply.

I didn't tell them what happened or what the note said. It was a secret.

4
Joys of Childhood

One day daddy brought home two walking dolls, both just about my height. Since I had no siblings, I did everything with those dolls. I put on their pajamas when we went to bed, combed their hair in the morning, and dressed them. Mommy and I bought clothes for them at the same store that my clothes came from. I don't think I'd be exaggerating to say they were the best-dressed dolls in the whole Crown Heights.

My life-size doll and me

Somewhere around the time, I turned five; I came up with the idea I could grow watermelons in Carmel. So months before leaving for the summer, I asked anyone who ate watermelon at our house to save the seeds for me. I washed them, dried them, and stored them in a jar that in the end came with me to Carmel.

The big tree outside the kitchen window seemed to be the right place to put my idea to work. It kept the kitchen cool and had a good size circle of soil around the trunk. One morning I took my jar of seeds and a shovel and headed out the door. Stooping next to the tree, I dug small holes in which I placed the seeds, circling the tree. Suddenly, I heard mommy's voice from the kitchen.

"Well, what are we going to grow?" Mommy asked.

"Watermelon," I called back.

"Good luck! You sure chose an odd spot to grow watermelon. But if we get any, I'm sure it will be the best I've eaten," declared mommy getting back to her chores.

I didn't realize then that the tree would block the sun, and there was little chance that anything would grow. So much for growing watermelon! It was a fun venture anyway, and for a young child that's all that mattered.

Aside from doing silly things, summers in Carmel with mommy were never dull. It was when most of our mother-daughter conversations took place.

On hot days, mommy and I sat under the umbrella on the back patio in the shade of the blue spruce tree. She'd tell me stories about things I did when I was a baby or toddler.

"When you were six months old, you loved playing peek-a-boo with your rubber squeeze doll," Mommy said. "You were definitely a doll lover. You had many of them and the collection seemed to grow as you did."

"How many?"

"Do you think I ever counted them? A whole shelf full in the city, and more here."

"What else did I do?"

"You loved books. You weren't the typical bookworm who enjoys and sometimes 'reads' books between the age of three or four. I read to you all the time. You had shelves full of books. Sometime between six to eight months, you leafed through books for the pictures. Never tore a page or scribbled them. In fact, even in your coloring books, daddy brought you from the store, you worked hard to keep the color within the lines. Your patience was unusual for a child your age. As you got older, you no longer had to be perfect. As long as you did your best, it was fine with you and us," she went on.

"I love books."

"I know. That's why I read them to you."

"Anything else?"

"When you were a year old, we gave you a stuffed "Lambchop," the little lamb from 'The Shari Lewis Show' on TV. You loved it very much and held it in your hand as you stumbled while learning to walk. Watching you waddle around with Lambchop was a pleasant sight and made me feel good."

"I loved Lambchop. Where is he now?"

"I don't know, but when we go home we'll look for him, okay?"

"Okay." I climbed off her lap and ran off to play.

"I'll go get us some lunch."

"Gloria, get up! We have lots to do today," Mommy shouted from the kitchen.

"I'm getting up, but what is so important that we have to do today?" I called back.

Coming into my room, mommy walked over and helped me get dressed. "We're going shopping to get you new clothes and supplies for school. Next week is September and you'll be starting kindergarten at PS 189. You'll meet new friends and your teacher will teach you lots of new things."

The first day of school arrived. All my friends were walking to school with their mothers, and mommy was walking me, too. PS 189 was a rectangular, flat-roofed, three- or four-story brick building with a huge yard. Outside it looked old and uninviting, but inside the place came alive. The hustle and bustle of hundreds of children, eager to find their classrooms and meet their new teachers, filled the hallways throughout the building. The rushing of teachers to their classrooms and parents stopping to chat with friends, neighbors, and newcomers portrayed a busy morning where chaos would lead to organized classes in session. My teacher was Ms. Adler, a young lady who greeted us with a smile. She moved around the room gracefully, stopping by each student, laying her hand gently on his or her shoulder asking us our names. She made me feel important, and I liked her a lot, right from the start.

There were only thirteen other children in my class. Sharing my class were my friend Melody, and my neighbors Lawrence and Rocky, so we walked to school and back home together. It was fun to trudge through the park every day with my friends and trudged through the snow when it snowed. Our footsteps left a trail of deep holes showing the path we took.

The daily schedule at school was chaotic, but we survived. First thing in the morning, Ms. Adler collected "milk money," the quarters that covered the cost of a small container of ice-cold milk and tempting cookies served during snack time. The recitation of the Pledge of Allegiance followed. After that came a variety of subjects: reading, writing, arithmetic, penmanship, spelling, history, and science (animals), sometimes interrupted by a fire drill once a month. Noisy voices erupted in the hallway as we scampered to exit the building, as fast as we could. The fire drill offered students a change of pace. Our school days included extra stuff, too, like IQ tests, reading tests, Health Day, and the annual spelling bee.

Besides school, mommy registered me for tap dance lessons once a week with Ms. Sharley, a middle-aged unmarried woman who loved children. Her studio was a huge room, with round bars lining the walls we used for ballet. We'd wear leotards and tutus and ballet slippers for ballet, changing into tap shoes (black shoes with metal plates on the heels) for the tap dance section of the lesson.

"Good afternoon, my wonderful darlings," she'd greet us as we arrived for our lesson.

"Good afternoon Ms. Sharley," we shouted as we hurried in to get ready.

"Let's see who I'm missing today," she'd take attendance. "Gather 'round the piano for our warm-up."

Warm-up with Ms. Sharley was fun. She played songs she taught us, and we'd accompany her by singing them. Sometimes she'd quiz us.

"Who can tell me what song this is?" She asked playing a piece.

"How Much Is that Doggy…," we'd shout out together.

"Wonderful," she said. "What about this one?"

"My Favorite Things."

"My, oh my! Looks like you've been doing homework. That was wonderful. Shall we get dancing?"

"Yippee! Tap and ballet," we shouted getting into place on the floor.

"Okay, let's start with a review of what we learned last week in tap, and I'll teach you something new in ballet today."

When the lesson ended, we left shouting a great big "bye Ms. Sharley, see ya next week."

In June, I turned six and as soon as school let out for the summer, mommy and I left for Carmel. That second Friday seemed as if mommy was in more of a rush to finish her chores earlier than usual.

"Why are you in such a hurry?" I asked.

"Daddy is coming earlier today; he wants to take us somewhere tomorrow."

"Where are we going?"

"Daddy wants to take us to Hyde Park, President Roosevelt's home, and burial place."

Daddy's coming earlier for the weekend and the upcoming trip to Hyde Park was such great excitement I couldn't sit still. I turned on my record player and put on vibrant music to dance around like a little butterfly fluttering in the air with wings. My arms, or should I say wings, spread out as I skipped around in no particular order, as I tried to keep up with the rhythm. It wasn't too long before Daddy's car pulling into the driveway drowned the sound of the music. I turned off my record player and flew out the door to greet him.

"Daddy, are we really going to Hyde Park?" I asked with disbelief. Other than Lakewood and Coney Island I had been nowhere else, so this was a real treat.

"Yep, and not only that but tomorrow night, now that you're old enough, we'll take you to the Annual County Carnival on the banks of Lake Gleneida in town."

"Is that why all my friends are here this weekend?"

"I suppose so."

I loved Hyde Park with its vast grassy lawns overlooking the Hudson River. We spent the day there, taking walks and picnicking on the lawn for lunch. Then we headed back to Carmel, so we'd be on time for a fun night at the carnival.

Saturday evening came and our division of five houses looked deserted as everyone left for a night in town. The sight was something to see. The carnival placed a huge Ferris wheel in the center of the lawn at the entrance to town. There were also lots of other amusement rides, arcades, and entertainment. The mixed aromas of freshly prepared foods rose into the air encouraging people to buy. Most popular, amongst the young ones, was the cotton candy, but they also had barbecued burgers, hot dogs, and tempting corn on the cob. During this weeklong carnival, the town came alive. From that day on, I went to the carnival every year with my friends, and we had lots of fun. It was a great way to end the summer before heading back to the city for another year of school.

Shortly after school began, losing my first baby tooth once again reminded me I was different. Or was I? I don't know. Perhaps I was confused rather than different. Sadly, unlike my friends and most other children, I didn't know about the tooth fairy (and my parents, being old school, probably didn't either) as she never visited me to leave money under my pillow. But that didn't stop my teeth from falling out with new permanent ones replacing them.

Me at six and toothless holding my first dog, Scotty

It was now I got my first pet, a black and white cocker spaniel. I named him Scotty. Scotty scared me because he was all jumpy and I didn't want him to jump on me, but he later became my best friend. The first night Scotty was home, I climbed onto the table in the hallway where the phone sat in one corner. I sat shaking like the small tremors following an earthquake and ready to burst into tears. Scotty positioned himself head turned up toward me with a pleading look in his eyes, as if planning a strategy to jump up and reach the top of the table, begging me to come down and play with him.

"Aren't you going to get off that table?" Mommy called from the kitchen.

"No, I'm too scared of Scotty," I called back. But before long, the inevitable happened—I needed to use the bathroom. I faced a dilemma. Will fear and the embarrassment of peeing in my pants win or will the courage to descend from the table and walking to the bathroom with Scotty close behind win? I made a quick decision that fear will not win and slowly descended from the table and tiptoed to the bathroom with Scotty following right behind me. He did not jump on me, and I got in and closed the bathroom door. Now the only thing separating Scotty and me was the closed door. Scotty lay down outside the door, whimpering while waiting for me to come out. You know the line from a show that goes "A funny thing happened on the way to..." In my case, it was ... to the bathroom. I realized that since Scotty didn't jump or growl at me there was nothing to fear. I could be friends with him. It would even be fun to be friends with him. When I opened the door, Scotty looked up at me sadly seeming to ask if I would consider being his friend. "Oh, you cute little thing," I said, "You look so sad. I'll be your friend if you won't jump on me."

Scotty got up wagging his tail, came up and licked my hand as if to say, "Okay." Soon after, I returned from school one day and noticed it was quieter than usual. I didn't hear the pitter-patter of tiny dog paws in the hallway coming to greet me.

"Scotty," I called. "Where are you?"

Mommy came to the door, "Scotty got sick and is gone." Tears streamed down my cheeks. *No, this couldn't be. He was okay this morning.*

"What happened to him?"

"Scotty came down with rabies, and I had to call the ASPCA to come take him away," mommy explained.

Suddenly, I missed Scotty. Now, no one followed my footsteps with a wagging tail. I cried. From that moment on, I knew I was in love with dogs.

I told mommy, "I want to get another dog." Mommy looked at me sadly, hugged me, and went back to her chores.

5
More Memories

Two years had passed. I was now in third grade, and my teacher was Mrs. Gardner, a grandmother type. She was older than most teachers were, wore glasses, and always had a hug ready for any of her charges that needed one. She spoke in a soft voice and praised us when we answered something correctly or had outstanding results on homework assignments. Though the work was super easy for me, I still got a great deal of her praise. I wasn't homeschooled, but the nursery school and kindergarten I attended did a fantastic job of prepping me for elementary school. First and second grade are too soon to tell how advanced a student is. But by the time I hit third grade, it showed.

"The academic level isn't high enough to challenge Gloria," she told my parents one day. Mommy and daddy took her advice. A short time later, they transferred me to the Beth Rivkah School for Girls, a private school run by the Orthodox Chabad movement. The school was right next door to daddy's store, which made it very convenient. My family wasn't Orthodox, and daddy kept his store open on Saturdays. The principal knew of this from the start. No one objected, and everyone else welcomed me. I made many good friends and stay in contact with some of them to this day.

The only problem we had to put up with were the ultra-orthodox members of our community who objected. They would yell out to us "Shame on you! Disgracing Shabbos!" while on their way home from the synagogue as they passed mommy and me doing our shopping. We acted as if we didn't know whom they were talking to. But, I dreaded going back to school on Sundays, always afraid someone would bring it up. Thankfully, no one ever did. And yes, I said Sundays. Since this was an Orthodox school, we attended a half-day on both Friday and Sunday.

That spring we went on a family trip abroad to Europe and Israel. We sailed on a huge cruise ship. Mommy's cousin Rochelle Tarner joined us for the trip. We stopped at ports in Portugal and Italy on the way. I had a horrible case of motion sickness and spent most of the trip in our cabin. Two special moments of the trip stuck in my mind.

The first was the escape drill. The shrilling siren sounded and the crew members told us to "Get your life jackets on now." Seeing everyone in bright orange air-filled life jackets parading around the deck brought an image of us ending up in the ocean. Not knowing how to swim, I didn't trust the life jackets. It frightened me. From one perspective it looked like a parade of two-footed jack-o-lanterns strolling along the deck, on another, it looked like a bunch of passengers in trouble awaiting their only chance of survival.

The captain noticed me, took my hand and in a calm voice said, "Don't be afraid. This is only a drill. The chance of something happening is small."

Hearing that from someone who had been through this routine many times calmed me. My heart stopped racing, the butterflies in my stomach stopped dancing, and the shaking subsided.

The second was the talent show. Mommy signed me up to perform. She dressed me in a Romanian embroidered jacket and hat set, a family heirloom for many years; no one seemed to know where it originated. I did a tap dance and sang—"How Much Is That Doggy in the Window." It surprised me to learn that the first place award would be mine for the taking. The ship's photographer took a picture of me with the head stewardess and later the captain shook my hand.

Shaking hands with the Captain after winning first prize in the talent show

Uncle Caesar was like a second father. He was the greatest uncle a child could want, and he gave me my nickname, Gaudy. Uncle Caesar was the only one I let call me Gaudy. I always thought it originated from my pronunciation of the title of my favorite book, Goody: the Mother Cat. Elisa later told me my pronunciation of my name earned me the title. How Gloria became Gaudy is beyond my grasp, but that doesn't matter. What matters is that it became a symbol of our loving bond. Later that year cousin Elisa got married. It was a beautiful affair, and I liked Michael, her new husband, The hall was huge, and the crew had the tables covered in white tablecloths with colorful mixes of flowers in vases set in the middle of the table.

Sometime between Elisa's wedding and October 1964, a new family, the Kellman's, arrived from Tashkent, Azerbaijan and contacted daddy. They had a daughter, Bina, but we had a hard time communicating. She didn't speak English, and I didn't speak Russian. This presented my first challenge of teaching English as a second language. I began by pointing to things and telling her the English word for each item. Bina was a quick learner and could soon speak with me. Daddy helped her father get started in his business by setting him up with a stand, at the market near our store, selling fabrics. This venture led to a successful textile business in Manhattan that continued to grow and prosper.

When I was ten, I met Elma, my first black friend. We

met by talking to each other through the window as we ate our meals. She lived in a private home behind our apartment building, and our kitchen windows faced each other. Her family always dressed well and seemed well situated. This was important to write about as this was a time when an apartment came available in our neighborhood black families from poorer areas came in as tenants. Not all of these families wanted to live in peace with the remaining white residents. Burglaries increased, muggings slowly became a common event, and long-time friends formed cliques so we didn't have to mingle with the newcomers. I invited her to my birthday party along with my other friends from my building. Sadly, our friendship ended when her family moved out of the area as did many other old-time residents. We stayed on for a while longer.

One day that summer mommy and I went to the butcher to get some meat. She noticed a sign that said he had puppies available. Jokingly, mommy asked him "with the meat or without?" I ended up with my second dog, Queenie, a fox terrier mix whom I cherished. Queenie was white with a brown spot covering the left half of her face and left ear. I was no longer scared like I was with Scotty. We became good friends. We loved playing ball, and Queenie was the best catcher. I'd throw one, and she'd catch it in her mouth. Looking back now, I am horrified at some of the things my friends and I did to her. One of them was when we tried to teach her to walk on two feet by putting her into a baby walker. Queenie was also spoiled. Every summer we celebrated her birthday by hosting a party, with hats and all, to which we invited all of our neighbors. She was a true friend and a lucky dog having lived with us both in the United States and in Israel. She died of heart failure at sixteen after surviving three surgeries for benign tumors.

My dog Queenie

Several weekends in Carmel that summer, as Queenie and I romped around on the grass, daddy and Uncle Caesar built me a full-size playhouse up on the hill. They even put screens in the windows to keep out the bugs, and they put a real lock on the door. I loved playing there with my friends. We decorated it, put up curtains, and painted the outside. It even had a sign out front that said, "Gloria's Motel." Reading all the articles today about the tiny houses brings back memories of this playhouse. All that was missing were an actual kitchen and bathroom. I took care of sleeping arrangements by having a cot and a doll's crib. This turned out to be the last project and the last thing daddy ever built for me though neither daddy nor Uncle Caesar knew that. These two men had hands of gold, loved cooking up projects and going at them, though not all of them succeeded. In that case came the challenge of making the project work. Some clever solutions cropped up in thosc days.

The house that daddy and Uncle Caesar built for me in Carmel, New York

6
Spirit in the Sky

The first time I encountered death, I was in the fifth grade.

It was Wednesday, June 9, 1966, when my friend Melody invited me to spend the weekend with her and her family. We had spent many weekends with each other's families, so I had no reason to believe this one should be different. Saturday was my eleventh birthday. But, with no party planned, I thought spending time with my friend could be fun. My parents agreed, and so I got ready to go to Melody's house on Friday morning.

On Thursday evening, daddy came home sick from work. He looked as white as a ghost did, and his skin was sweaty. I didn't know he was having a heart attack, nor did I know what brought it on. I didn't know that until many years later. What I knew was that on Thursday the medics took daddy to the hospital by ambulance for treatment to help him get better. Melody's mother picked me up the next morning to go to Melody's house for the weekend.

Everything fell into place: Melody's family cared for me over the weekend, mommy had the time to spend with daddy in the hospital, and daddy had the best of care in the hospital. Still a strange feeling was taking hold of me. The whole situation confused me. What made daddy sick? Why on my birthday weekend?

We awoke early on Sunday and after getting our breakfast headed off to have fun.

Melody's parents planned to surprise me with a small birthday party that morning before I went home. That morning, as usual, Melody, her brother Mick, and I were playing pretend games, as we loved doing. This time, we were a Pilgrim family living in Colonial America.

Then the phone rang, and Melody's mom answered. It was mommy calling to tell her the shocking news.

Melody's mom came to the door and said, "Gloria, get dressed. I need to take you home now. Your mother needs you."

Needing to go home unexpectedly confused me. What happened to the birthday party Melody's family had planned? I felt cheated. It wasn't fair. Why was mommy doing this? She knew we were having fun, and I was okay. Why did she call and order me to come home for no reason? Or was there a reason that nobody told me?

Mommy met me at the door and said, "We will see Dr. Bloch now." She took me by the hand, locked the door, and we were off to walk the block and a half to my pediatrician's office.

As a healthy eleven-year-old, none of this made much sense, but I went. Dr. Bloch took me into his office and let me sit on my favorite musical chair. He gave me a doll to hold while talking with me. He told me that daddy was sick, and the doctors at the hospital did everything they could to help him get better. Sometimes it doesn't work out that way. Sometimes people just do not have the willpower or strength to fight their illnesses. He ended with "I'm sorry, but your daddy died last night."

My reaction: stunned, shocked, speechless. Life was not supposed to be this way. It was my birthday. I should have been celebrating, if not with my family, at least with my friends. Instead, I sat there, staring into space. This just turned into the worst day of my young life, and one that added anger (why did I have to be dragged to my doctor on a weekend, and on my birthday to boot?) and hurt (tears streamed down my cheeks) to my already sensitive soul. Though I didn't realize it then, I was angry with mommy.

To this day, I still feel hurt and deprived of the right to have grieved for the only daddy I knew. Why? What would cause a mother not to be able to face her child in times of tragedy? Why could she, herself, not tell me of daddy's death? Did mommy expect me, an eleven-year-old child, to be the strong one? While no one was there to comfort me, did mommy expect me to comfort her? These are questions that have followed me since that day, and there are others too. Unfortunately, I will never know the answers. Somehow, I had the strength to fulfill the expectations of others.

Because daddy had no sons, the group of at least ten men needed in Orthodox Judaism to form a Minyan, did not meet daily to say special prayers during the week of Shiv'ah, the period in which the mourning family wears dark clothing and sits on the floor. People who knew daddy came to visit and offered their condolences. Some brought food for my grieving family.

Many visitors came to comfort mommy, but she and my

aunts and uncles kept me in my room and allowed out only for meals. It made me feel as though I wasn't part of the family. I knew they meant it for my own good. I was too young in their eyes to witness grief. It was an attempt to shield me from this. I had a daddy whom they didn't allow me to grieve for; and a father I never knew who died before my learning who he was and so once again not having the chance to grieve over his death. My aunts and uncles fed me in the kitchen and that was the only time I had to be with them. They were there mainly to see I had eaten, done my homework and got to sleep on time. The rest of the time, they mingled with the guests coming to pay a visit to my mourning mommy. My cousins came to visit with me in my room from time to time and we played games or read books together.

I remember how strange the house looked and felt. Mommy had covered the mirrors and paintings with white sheets as is done in the Jewish faith when a person passes away. The television and radio were silenced for the whole week. Mommy dressed in black and continued to dress in this fashion for the first year. Since no one told me what to expect to an eleven-year-old this seemed odd, but I did as the adults told me, and life went on.

Mommy took over running the store, and I joined the ranks of latchkey kids. I hated coming home from school to an empty house and complained. Mrs. Auburn, one of daddy's customers, was now working in the store because she owed a debt and was paying it off in labor. She suggested to mommy that she work part of the day in the store, and then to go to our apartment to care for me after school. We did that until my friends begged me to come to their houses after school to play and do homework together. Mommy agreed, and I went to a different friend each day. Mrs. Auburn returned to the store full time.

That summer, my friend Melody and I went to the Hi-Li Day Camp on Long Island. Mommy dropped me off at Melody's house in the morning and the bus picked us up in the morning and brought us back to her house in the afternoon. Of the twenty-eight girls in our group, the only one I remember is Melody, perhaps because I already knew her and was not into socializing much only a month after daddy's death. Memories from camp are vague. The specifics are not there, but I guess we played games and did arts and craft projects. Isn't that what kids do at camp? There are no recollections of what the place looked like in my mind, so one could probably say I was still in shock and in my own world that summer from all that had occurred.

Many things that happened since daddy's passing became a blank void in my mind as I remember little, nor do I remember clearly, what it was like with daddy. The shock of daddy's sudden passing and not experiencing the opportunity to grieve caused a memory lapse, if that is even possible. I know that a big gap exists in my memory for daddy from the Thursday he left for the hospital and the period after his passing. As the saying goes "Life goes on," so on with life I went.

By the time, I started sixth grade that fall, Beth Rivkah had moved to Ocean Avenue in the Flatbush section of Brooklyn,

New York. My school was now split into two buildings. The building on the corner of Church Avenue and Ocean Avenue, abutting the yard of Erasmus High School on Flatbush Avenue, housed the elementary and middle school. Our high school was one block down, on the opposite corner. I could no longer go with mommy in the morning, go to school, and then spend the afternoon at the store. To get to school and home I had to take public transportation and hated it from the start. The high school kids took the same bus or train back and forth from school as a number of my friends and I did, but unlike us who bothered no one, the other kids bullied us. Not a day went by without some incident occurring (bus passes stolen, someone beat up, others called names, etc.)

April 1967 brought my first Passover holiday without daddy. Aunt Ruth and Uncle Caesar hosted the Seder during the Passover meal, where we recount the story of the Jewish nation exiting Egypt at their house. The whole family was there. Uncle Caesar led the Seder. Since I was the youngest one present, I had the honor of asking the Four Questions, known as the Mah Nishtahnah. As I recited them, I felt the presence of daddy, now a spirit in the sky watching over me.

Two months later, I turned twelve. This was the year I would celebrate my Bat Mitzvah and take on the status of a woman. From this point on, I would bear the responsibility for my own wrongdoings. Since this was also the first anniversary of daddy's death, there was no big party planned. Instead, I had a quiet birthday party at home with some of my good friends.

Mommy set up the children's table in the living room, and

My Bat-Mitzvah party at home with some good friends

the adult buffet, for my aunts and uncles, in an adjoining bedroom. We had kosher pizza delivered, so my Orthodox friends could eat, too, and used paper plates and cups and plastic spoons for the cake. What I missed was the music. Technically, we were still within the year of mourning when we held the party so there could be no music. And that brought me to thinking about my piano lessons.

I started piano in first grade at school. Looking back, I don't see how anyone can learn to play anything using a long sheet of paper with the piano keyboard printed on it. But that's how my piano experience began. When daddy died, I already had a private teacher who came to my house after school for an hour each week. After daddy died, I almost gave up studying piano. I hated my teacher so much because she always pulled my ears before she left to make sure I would practice. Give me a break! Like that would help motivate me to practice. To prevent me from stopping altogether, mommy found a very nice Romanian teacher, Mrs. Mona, and I studied with her. I liked her a lot, and whatever little I still remember I learned with her.

In September 1968, I had my first piano concert at Mrs. Mona's home. There were fifteen students, all girls, and our parents. We each played one or two pieces and Mrs. Mona treated us to refreshments at the end.

During 1968, mommy and I went to Paris and Israel. In Paris, I met my relatives, Annette and Boris Feldman, and their daughter Heugette. Sophie and Dani her children came with her. Sophie must have been around three or four years old. Later, as a teenager, Sophie, having moved with her family to Israel, would one day live close by to us and babysit my oldest son, Chanan, in Tel Aviv.

Boris Feldman was a great pianist. He and his wife Annette owned a restaurant in the Paris countryside with outdoor seating where he would entertain while his wife, Annette, served the dinners.

In Israel, I met my mother's cousins and friends. After a

wonderful trip, we returned home. During the summer of 1968 I wasn't looking for a job, but the Chabad Day Camp for Boys, in Brooklyn, New York offered me a position as an assistant counselor in the preschool group, which I accepted. We were five counselors altogether. The head counselor was Jody. The two assistant counselors were Marilyn and I. Jody's sister, Stella, and another girl were junior aides. Our group comprised twenty-one three to five-year-olds. There were two boys, both three years old, whom I remember well. One was Azriel Osage, who seemed to like me and followed me wherever I went. He was a thumb-sucker and needed warm, individual attention, which I gave him. The other one was Seth Davis. He was quiet and shy at the beginning, partly because it was his first time away from his parents for the whole day.

Since these two boys were always with me, they became good friends and soon left my side to go play together, one day joining in with the rest of the group. This was a great satisfaction for me to see how they developed in such short time.

In September, it was back to school. I was in eighth grade and that year I would graduate from middle school and get ready to enter high school. The year was uneventful, and before I knew it, another school year passed and summer of 1969 arrived. Graduation Day came to signal the end of eight years of schooling and the commencement of another four years of high school. There was a big ceremony and my guests included my relatives, friends, cousins, Stevonna, Melody, Mick, and some other friends.

About a week later, I met with other young teens at

Devorah Majeski and I at our eighth grade graduation

Kennedy Airport for a flight to Israel ending at Kfar Silver in Ashkelon. This was a six-week camp organized by the Zionist Organization of America. We were thirty-eight teens from all over the U.S.A. It was fun, and I have a few special memories left from that summer. One was when the boys played a trick on us by locking my roommates and me in our room. After a while, they set us free. Another time when we were visiting a kibbutz and working in the tomato fields, the boys threw tomatoes at the girls. This time, we fought back, and we were one bunch of messy teens when we got back from the fields. No one won, but we all had fun.

I loved Kfar Silver so much I hoped to go back the following year to study at the American school there. Little did I know then, the impact this would have on me later. In the meantime, I was about to enter high school and get back into my routine.

7
High School and the Big Move

Another school year began along with piano lessons and dreams of returning to Kfar Silver. The highlight of my first year in high school was my class's April Fool's Day trick we planned for our history teacher, as I recall it. No one in the class liked her very much because she yelled at us often, so we chose her as our victim. We put water in a small pail and set it on a ledge above the door. We tied one end of a string to the pail's handle and the other end to the doorknob. When our teacher entered the water would pour over her, but things didn't always end up with the planned result. This was one such time.

For this reason or other, our teacher was running late that morning, so our principal entered our classroom instead. She intended to get us started on some work. Mind you, we hadn't accounted for this possibility. We sat there with bulging eyes and mouths wide open taking in the scene as our bucket of water soaked our well-liked principal. Luckily, she accepted the circumstances and remained calm; though I can't be sure, she didn't have a good talk with her granddaughter, a member of our class.

Towards the spring, I acted on the possibility of attending Kfar Silver for my sophomore year. Mommy agreed on one condition: she could act as a chaperone for the group on the flight over, and stay in a rented apartment for the year. We found out that her cousins wanted to rent their Tel Aviv apartment, and the administrative staff accepted her chaperone offer. Preparations began. Mommy listed the store for sale.

Leaving during the summer of 1970 meant I would miss my Sweet Sixteen party and the opportunity to say goodbye to many good friends. Mommy found a solution. She combined both the Sweet Sixteen and a Bon Voyage into one big, early celebration. That resulted in the biggest party I ever had. Fifteen to twenty friends besides relatives attended. Mommy had arranged for my Masada youth group leader to come play his accordion for us. It was both fantastic and sad. I didn't want it to end.

Finally, the end of the school year arrived and with preparations well under way for our trip to Israel, we had little to do except to pack. Because I would receive all the books I'd need at a school in Kfar Silver, I only packed winter and summer clothes to last the year. Since mommy would stay in Tel Aviv for the year, I took only summer clothes with me and packed my winter things with mommy's stuff. I'd take the warmer clothes later when the weather turned colder. With August fast approaching, we visited with family members to say goodbye. Like with my friends, I lost contact with many of my cousins, but, mostly reestablished contact later through Facebook online. Now all grown up with families of our own we continue to keep in touch through this venue.

In August, we boarded the plane to Israel. I stayed in Tel Aviv with mommy in the rented apartment, which belonged to mommy's cousin Clara and her husband, until school started in September.

I made friends with a girl named Goldie who lived a block away and with Kevin, who visited for the summer and was staying with his grandparents, neighbors in the same building we lived in. Kevin was from Melbourne, Australia. The three of us spent time together like the Three Musketeers. Soon Kevin went back home, and I left for Kfar Silver. I continued to see Goldie on the weekends when I came home to visit.

Once again, things didn't turn out as planned. I went off to the American school in Kfar Silver expecting it to be like the summer I spent there. Boy, was I in for a culture shock! Ninety-nine percent of the students at the school came from broken home environments, something with which I had no experience. Coming from a good, stable environment, this hit me hard. I had trouble connecting with my fellow students and felt lonely and miserable. But since it was my idea, I would tough it out for the year.

By October, luck was on my side. I developed an infection in my mouth. While I visited mommy for the Succot holiday, she decided not to let me stay there for the year, but she didn't tell me about her plan. After the holidays, I returned to school. Within a few days, the teacher asked me to go to the office. Waiting for me in the office were mommy and an acquaintance of ours. She told me I'd go home with her, and I should go get my stuff. As though a bolt of lightning struck me, I flew out of there, into my room, packed and was ready to go in less than thirty minutes. I couldn't believe it. Words can't describe the happiness I felt that day.

I transferred to the Gymnasium "Herzliya" High School in Tel Aviv after we remained in Israel through the end of the year. This was the elite of high schools in the area, and not everyone could get in. There I met six other English-speaking natives. Together we came from three different countries: the U.S.A., Australia, and South Africa. We became friends and stuck together, supporting and encouraging each other when our studies got tough, which occurred most of the time.

Since we were a large group, the school organized special tutoring for us during the English lessons. The hardest part that year centered on the need to catch up in French since my placement was in the French-English bilingual section. This meant I had to pass both matriculation exams with good scores to graduate, yet the class had already studied French for two years and was well into its third year. I, however, had never studied French and had just learned Hebrew. Talk about tough times. *How did they expect me to learn three years of French in one while learning Hebrew at the same time? Two languages, as different as day and night, in one year. One of them, for the matriculation exam in June.* My teacher offered to tutor me, so twice a week I would board the bus after school for the half-hour ride to get to her house for lessons. It paid off as I took the matriculation exam with the class at the end of the year, earning a passing grade of seven.

I also required tutoring in math, or more precisely, trigonometry, as I never took geometry. This meant I went from algebra straight to trigonometry, itself a big jump, made more difficult because Hebrew was the language of instruction.

To make life easier, mommy and the school's administrative staff decided that I had to repeat eleventh grade, enabling me to take the English and Hebrew matriculation exams needed for graduation. This made sense as when I entered the school instead of placing me in tenth grade—my actual grade level—they had placed me into eleventh grade. *Hmmm... didn't I say we were there for a year? What happened to that?* This decision put an end to returning to the States at the end of the year. We stayed in Israel, and I continued the next year at the same school.

During the summer, I remained in Israel with family friends, while mommy went home to pack the rest of our belongings left in the Brooklyn apartment, and make other necessary arrangements before returning to Israel for an unknown length of time.

Upon mommy's return, she bought an apartment in a four-story apartment building with an elevator in Bavli, a section of Tel Aviv, on the banks of the Yarkon River. There were three apartments on each floor. Mommy bought a second-floor apartment that faced the front, overlooking the street and the park alongside the river. The apartments were rectangular. Ours was on the left side of the hallway, to the right of the elevator. The entry door opened into the dining area, which opened into the living room. At the far right end of the living room, sliding doors led to the balcony. At the far left side of the dining area, a door led to the small, square kitchen. With not much storage space, mommy had an added stand-alone cabinet built to match the ones between the kitchen, and placed it in the refrigerator and the existing cabinets. For a table, she had a custom-ordered fold-down table attached to the opposite tiled wall.

At the other end, parallel to the entry door, another door led to the utility balcony used mainly for storage. Blinds on the outside wall of the balcony gave access to the outdoor clothes drying area. Although the balcony area was narrow, it had two more doors, one going to the bathroom and another to my bedroom. The narrow and long bathroom contained a separate shower, a bathtub, sink, and the washing machine. The toilet, in a tiny room of its own, had a door off the hallway between the bathroom and the entrance to my bedroom. Mommy had a closet custom-built in my bedroom on one of the longer walls leaving enough space for a pull-out sofa bed where I slept. Along the other wall, a bookshelf from floor to ceiling with an area cut out for a desk matched the closet. But I didn't place my desk there, as I needed room for my piano. Instead, my big, bulky custom-built desk went against the far wall near the window. Mommy's bedroom had a custom-built closet installed along with an L-shaped mirror with drawers on the opposite wall. To the left, a door led to another balcony with a storage closet. That's where I spent the next fourteen years. Very different from the huge rooms in our apartment back in Brooklyn, but comfortable enough for the two of us.

Just below us lived a family with a young girl, Cayla, who spent several years living in Uganda and had returned to Israel not long before. Cayla and I became friends. Cayla attended the English school in Jaffa, a city outside Tel Aviv, so during the school year, we had little time to spend together. After we moved and settled in, the new school year began.

By the end of high school, two years later, I had taken matriculation exams in all the subjects. Now as seniors facing graduation, we had to turn seriously to our studies. I believe we supported each other, helped each other learn the material, and felt confident that we could pass the exams helped us overcome the challenges involved. In June, 1974, I graduated along with the rest of my class and received my diploma.

I spent the summer mostly reading and babysitting. My friends and classmates prepared for mandatory draft into the Israel Defense Forces. In between, we met, partied, and enjoyed the time we had together.

I also prepared, but not for the army, to enroll at the Tel Aviv University. Speaking fluent English and finding a hidden proven ability to learn foreign languages with ease, I studied Applied Linguistics. I wanted to be a teacher, my dream from way back when and thought that this could be a good base for a teaching program later. They accepted me into the Applied Linguistics program for the fall of 1974. I had to decide on the courses I wanted to take during my first year, but I had a lot of time for that. In the meantime, I kept busy with all the routine work involved to prepare for attending a school of higher education.

8
The Yom Kippur War (1973)

Just eight months prior to graduating from high school, Rosh Hashanah came and went. Families were preparing for Yom Kippur. No one had a clue that this one would be different from any other. That morning families dressed and headed to the synagogues throughout the country as they did every year.

All was quiet on the home front. The whole country shut down: no public transportation, no electronic broadcasts, and no services. Children filled the streets with their bikes. People gathered in synagogues for prayer. All seemed to be a usual Yom Kippur day.

Suddenly sometime between noon and two o'clock in the afternoon empty streets were replaced by cars collecting uniformed soldiers, many of whom were still in the synagogues immersed in prayer. They headed to bases around the country. Many didn't even have time to part from their families. War had erupted. I was scared, as I never had to experience war before. Would there be school? Would it be safe? Syrian and Egyptian armies launched a surprise attack on Israel. The miracle, to come three weeks later, was that all the Arab forces were defeated.

Through the grapevine, we got word that our former neighbor, a couple with a son in the building where we previously rented, received unwelcome news. The army reported their son as missing in action. The mood was dim. About a week later, they found his body. Their son would never come home again.

I was sad. I knew him, and this was the first time someone so young that I knew had died. This was my first experience with war and its dreadful outcomes. He wasn't the only one. Israel lost 2,689 soldiers in the three-week Yom Kippur war.

I can't be sure what the news back in the States was reporting, but I remember incoming calls from my aunts and uncles begging us to come back and get away from it all. I recall them telling us, "The streets of Tel Aviv are burning, we don't understand why you would want to stay?" This was untrue, of course, but how do you tell them this? The truth is even if we had wanted to, there was no way out. It made me feel trapped. No matter what, my destiny was set for me. Either I survived or not. Might as well use my time as best I could, so my friends and I volunteered our free time to help in whatever way we could. We helped deliver newspapers, helped play with the young ones whose fathers were away on the war front, helped the elderly shop for food, etc. And we went to school. All flights out of Tel Aviv were suspended. Air controllers only allowed El Al flights with volunteers from abroad to land, and they came in large numbers. Young adults, many students who took a leave from their studies, came to help the kibbutz movement with the apple harvest and other tasks.

I recall bits and pieces of the war days. Tel Aviv was blacked out. Headlights of cars and buses were painted blue. People with private cars drove the streets to help others get from one place to another. Buses were running but with a short supply of drivers.

I remember the second day all the neighbors gathered in the shelter to clean it up and set up places to sit and play corners for the young ones. It was a team effort, and though we all hoped we wouldn't need to use it, we all wanted it to be ready if we did. Later that day, the sirens came, and we all headed to the shelter. It was important to keep the little ones busy so we read them stories and helped them fall asleep. Though I was terrified, I could not show my fear. It would scare the younger ones so, like the adults, I had to be strong for them. Instead of breaking down, I went to help with the little ones. There were infants to feed, toddlers to keep busy, and older ones to care for. The all clear siren came hours later. We all returned to our apartments. Three weeks later the war was over. Life, having lost so many young men and women, was back to as normal as it could be.

Gloria Oren

9
My Stint in the Israeli Armed Forces

September 1974—I entered Tel Aviv University, located fifteen minutes from my home, to begin my academic studies. Unlike the teens of today, I didn't send out applications for scholarships. It wasn't something done there. Not having a clue what the cost was, or how it was paid, I suppose mommy covered the cost since my income from babysitting was little. Now knowing the true cost of higher education after having put three children through college I realize that even with the few scholarships they obtained, it was still quite pricey.

I majored in Applied Linguistics because it had to do with how languages developed, so it was probably a good start into the field of teaching English as a Second Language. An introduction to how languages developed would be a great help in understanding the difficulties encountered when learning a foreign language, especially in teaching English to Hebrew speakers. Besides, I had personal experience with learning foreign languages and knew first-hand the frustration involved.

Would I make the same choice today? No, as I haven't enjoyed anything I studied then. I would most likely have taken more language arts classes along with electives in education and teaching followed by a program meant to get a teacher's certificate.

My first friend, I made at the university was a wonderful girl from South Africa. We continued studying together until 1977 when the Israel Defense Forces caught up with me and announced in a letter I must enlist. Though I wasn't an Israeli citizen, living in Israel as an American citizen, it obligated me to serve through an agreement between Israel and the U.S.A. The army staff told me I could not volunteer to become an officer. I tried to get permission to continue my studies but to no avail. Three years of university and nothing to show is what I got instead. It upset me and angered me, but with time, I got over it. Oh well, that's life. I said goodbye to my friends and prepared for military training.

Of course, it could always be different. First, I could have returned home to the United States after high school and attended college there. But that would have changed my life. Most likely meaning I wouldn't have met and married my husband nor have had my three children with him. Perhaps someone else would have come along, but it's always hard to consider what could have been, as opposed to what is.

Leaving home was very hard for me because I had only been away for part of some summers in the past, but now I was off to training and didn't know if I'd be stationed close to home or whether I'd have to live on a military base. I couldn't prepare for this and was angry that I couldn't finish my studies. I didn't go willingly; it felt more as if the army forced me to do it when I had other plans. The injustice seemed even more heightened because my South African friends didn't have to serve in the military, but instead could continue their studies.

I arrived at the check-in center on the date given and was one of many other girls. Soldiers there gave us our uniforms, our injections, and told us to change our clothes. Then those in charge loaded us onto buses and took us to our base. We were there for two weeks.

One early morning around two o'clock a voice announced: "Wake up, inspection in two minutes."

Are they kidding me? I'm half-asleep. I don't need an inspection. We were to dress, grab our Uzis, and get out for an inspection; and we had two minutes to do so. We all got out on time and passed the inspection so we could get back to sleep for another few hours.

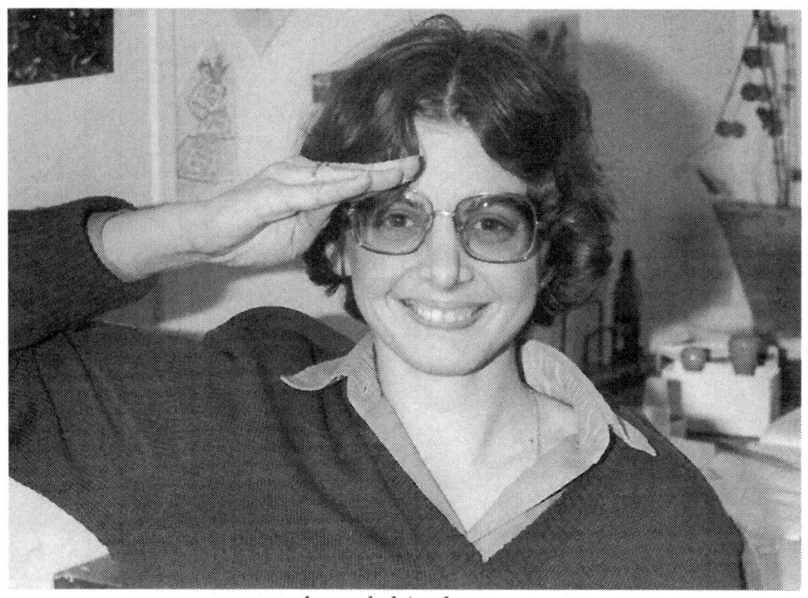

At my desk in the army

I didn't make friends with anyone during this period so parting at the end of the training session was easy. After training, they assigned me to a base in Tel Aviv, about twenty minutes from home.

My assignment was secretary to the Head of the Organization and Training Unit (also known as OHAD), which was a branch of the Army Spokesman's division. It was here that I became familiar with Reuters and the Associated Press news services.

One division in our unit was the liaison with the media, and it was in that office that all the soldiers in that unit fulfilled night duty on a rotating basis. We had a cot and attempted to get some sleep, but the faxes kept coming through the night. We had to make phone calls to discuss the urgent messages, and we also found time to party and have fun.

I was to replace a girl named Pleasant who was ending her service soon. Pleasant and I became good friends and continued our friendship until after we both married and went our own ways. She and her husband, Max, a pilot, moved to France. Years later, my husband and I, along with our two young sons, would move to the States.

Since I only knew how to type in English, my boss sent me to a typing class for Hebrew. After years of disorganization in the office, my job was to organize the file cabinets so that the officer or I could find something when we needed it. Besides that, I typed letters, as needed, prepared tea or coffee for my boss and his guests, washed the floor, answered the phone, and subbed for the Spokesman's typist when needed. Looking back now, I guess it wasn't as bad as I thought it would be. I made many good friends and gained the experience of working in an office doing many varied tasks. This experience, being a shy child, was a period of growth for me. It later helped me as an adult with children of my own. Sometimes I had to decide what to do or how to handle situations that arose, at times when my husband was away or otherwise unavailable. It forced me to step out of my shadow.

I was also the one chosen to run errands to the Chief of Staff's office, as no one else was brave enough to go there lest they chanced to meet him, Rafael Eitan, AKA Raful, face-to-face and would have to salute. No problem for me, though. One memorable incident comes to mind. One day while washing the floor with a sheet of plastic wrapped around me as an apron and latex gloves on my hands, Raful passed through the gate right near our office. So what did I do? I turned to him and with a rag in one hand, saluted with the other. It amazed everyone. I must admit it must have been quite a sight.

In my unit, I met Olga and Justin, both Americans, and we became known as the Three Musketeers. Also, in this unit, and destined to become good friends with me were Harry, the photographer who later took my wedding pictures, and Avery, who was the officer in charge of the reserves office for the unit. Avery was also Olga's boss. The three of us hung out a lot together.

Though not through the army, I met Tuvia, my future husband, in October 1979, and we dated. Tuvia's family arrived in Israel in 1960. By the time I met him, his family lived near Tel Aviv. We saw each other often, and I liked him a lot. I had hopes of getting married someday and saw a future with Tuvia.

I feared to have to leave mommy, as I was the only one she had left, but I knew it was time to move on and one day it would happen. In the meantime, I could only hope it would come soon, and I dreamed of our future together. Look, what else could a girl do? I couldn't force him to propose. With most of my classmates in the States marrying at eighteen, and some of my Israeli classmates marrying soon after release from the army I was feeling like a spinster. Will it ever happen? And when will it happen? How long would the wait be?

10
Alone and On My Own

On March 4, 1979, I took our white Peugeot 404 to work as mommy planned a day of cleaning. That afternoon, alone in the office, a neighbor called telling me to come home; mommy wasn't feeling well. I felt anxious, my body shaking, nervous what I would find. But I was in the army and couldn't just leave. So after arranging for someone to cover for me I headed home.

When I arrived home, an ambulance blocked the driveway to the parking lot behind the building. *Uh-oh, this isn't good. Something bad has occurred.* My neighbor waited in the entrance and took me straight to her apartment. She tried to prepare me for what was to come. I was scared, shaking, tears welling in my eyes, but the way my neighbors handled the situation was comforting.

Her husband came up from our apartment and from the look on his face; I sensed it was bad. No, make that more than bad. I will never forget the scene I saw just a few minutes later. When I entered our apartment, there was mommy lying on the tile floor near the dining room table, white as a ghost with no breath of life left in her. The medics said she died of a heart attack.

That was it. I was twenty-three, shaken up and alone, without parents or siblings in the world, or so I thought. I went into shock. No tears. No crying. Just shock. I sat there staring into space in the room oblivious to what was going on around me.

The medics gave me Valium to calm me down, and didn't leave me alone for one minute. When the medics were sure I'd be okay, they left. The morgue crew would soon come to take mommy away. Lying on the couch in shock, I didn't realize that mommy still had her gold wedding band on, and I never got it back.

Someone called several relatives, and they came, along with the other neighbors. They all meant well and were there to help me, but this was the most difficult time in my life, even more so than losing Daddy as a child. I didn't want them there, but how could I tell them that. All I wanted was to have the one person I cared most about, my boyfriend Tuvia, there with me to help me through this trying time. So they all stayed.

I called Tuvia and told him what happened. I asked him to come over as soon as he could. He arrived within a short time. He notified my dear Uncle Caesar who flew in from New Jersey three days later to be with me and attend the funeral. We had to call the funeral home and beg them to put off the burial until my uncle arrived, not an easy task as the Jewish tradition calls for burial within twenty-four hours. Due to the circumstances, they finally agreed. Uncle Caesar stayed for two weeks. He wanted me to go back to the States, and I did too, in some way, but what would I do, and where would I go? I wasn't emotionally able to make long-term decisions at the time and didn't want to make ones I'd later regret.

Another person worthy of mention and deserving of

thanks for all he did for me at this time of great loss in my life was my boss in the army, Lieutenant Colonel Abraham Alon. Lieutenant Colonel Alon helped guide me in arranging the funeral for mommy. A great boss and a good friend, I will always remember him.

Only later, our neighbors told me what took place that day. Mommy was cleaning and suddenly didn't feel well. She knocked on our next-door neighbor's door to tell them, and as she was about to close the door, she collapsed onto the floor. Besides the heart attack, I believe she may have fractured her skull as there was blood on her head, and she had fallen onto tile flooring. The authorities didn't note this on the death certificate.

It was too late now to have a heart-to-heart talk with mommy about my past. The realization that I would never know about my past had made dealing with mommy's death even harder. Questions surfaced once again. Why could she not have realized that I would need to know certain information, such as medical history, and she wouldn't be around forever to provide any clues? Was there anything specific she was trying to hide from me? What was she afraid of? Did she think I wouldn't love her anymore? It's now over thirty years since she passed away, and I love her as much as before even though I can't figure out why she was so secretive. The only explanation that makes sense is that some things are just not meant to be and others are.

I decided that I had to stay where I was. There were bank accounts to transfer and the title on the apartment and car and so on. I had a boyfriend I loved and felt I could trust, so I let him move in with me, even though we had no wedding planned. This was a major step for me as I had always believed I would wait until after getting married to have a male partner live with me under the same roof. I did maintain one condition to be strictly enforced, and that was that there was to be no sex at all. I didn't know then I'd be marrying in a short time and didn't want to face complicated issues. Let's not forget that I was an adoptee born out of wedlock, and I was determined not to repeat history. After a month of living together, we got married. No engagement ring. No formal engagement. Just a mutual decision to get married and the preparations began.

Map of Brooklyn, New York
1920–1957

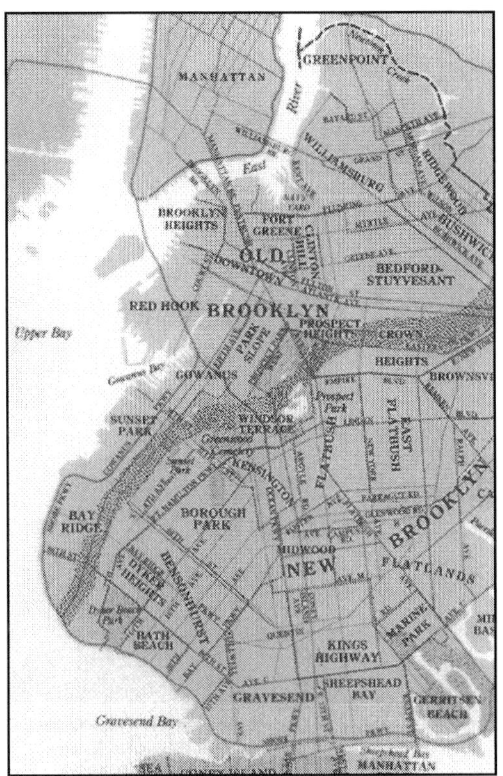

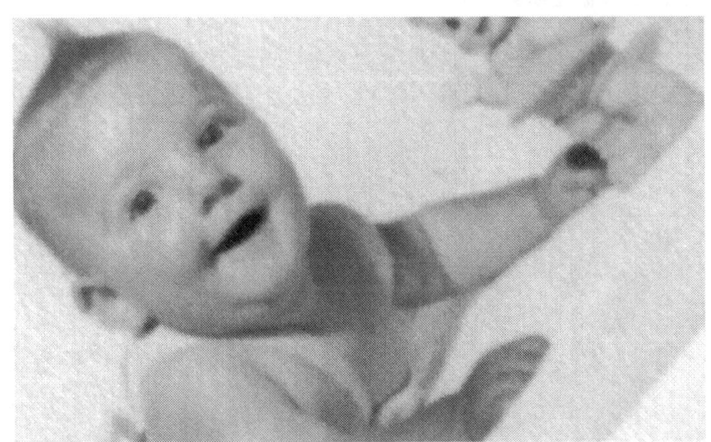

Me at 6 months

Daddy and I in the snow at Lincoln Terrace Park, Brooklyn, New York

The Beltzer outing at our house in Carmel, New York

Me at 18

Marcia as a teen

Aida Ross, my maternal biological grandmother

11
Married at Twenty-three

On May 14, 1979, just over two months since mommy passed away Tuvia, and I got married. This event turned me into a woman who would, G-d willing, raise her own family, and my priority of being the devoted daughter was changing to that of being the devoted wife. I don't believe I'd have agreed to get married had I felt I wasn't ready for it. Experiencing the reality of life has an impact on the individual. A person is born, raised to become a young adult, marries, perhaps raises his or her own family, and passes on. Those who are left must go on with their lives, and so it was to be.

It was a lovely wedding even without music due to the Jewish custom of a yearlong mourning period. Many people attended, including my military boss and his wife, and mommy's friend from New York, who was visiting relatives in Israel. Everyone was happy for me and glad to see me getting married. Not one person said anything about it being so soon after mommy's death. I was thankful for the many friends and relatives I had, and though I was at least technically an orphan I didn't feel alone.

Our honeymoon took us to Tiberias, a city in northern Israel, on the western shore of the Sea of Galilee, also known as Lake Kinneret. Tiberias, named after the Roman emperor Tiberius, who ruled from 14-37 CE, was a gift by Antipas, the son of King Herod. Tiberias, well known for its health and holiday resorts, many Jews also considered it a holy city and an important center of Jewish studies and culture. After the destruction of the Temples, during the second and third centuries, the Sanhedrin (Jewish council) moved to Tiberias. It was where the Mishnah—The Oral Jewish Law—was completed. Today Tiberias is a Jewish pilgrimage city—a center for tourism; famous Jewish Rabbis such as Rabbi Maimonides and Rabbi Akiva are buried there. We hung out at the pool, ate a fish dinner at a renowned restaurant on the shore of Lake Kinneret, and even visited Mount Tabor. It was wonderful. I enjoyed every minute. It was like living in a dreamland, a land where only smiles abound.

Soon after, I realized I was pregnant with our first child. I was twenty-three, and Tuvia was thirty. Though we were happy about becoming parents to a child of our own, it scared me, too. Being adopted I did not understand any possible health issues that may appear. When we finally told friends and family, that we were expecting, happiness filled the air.

We didn't make any special preparations while awaiting the arrival of our first child. I didn't have a baby shower. There's something about Jewish couples, having a baby, and inviting the evil eye. It's this something that lies behind the practice of not calling the child by name, referring to the child as "the baby," until the *Brit Milah* if it's a boy or the Baby Naming in the synagogue if it's a girl. It's this same something that prevents many Jewish couples from furnishing the room before the child's birth. Though we didn't furnish the room before our son's birth, we called him by his name after he arrived.

Our son, Chanan, born in the middle of February, was a wonderful Valentine's Day gift coming a day early. Since Chanan was born eleven months after mommy passed away, we had no problem deciding on a name. Her Hebrew name was Chanah, so we chose the male equivalent— Chanan— meaning G-d pardoned. The night before Chanan was born brings back old memories and a lesson to all first-time mothers. That evening I made fried zucchini fritters as a side dish for dinner with meat or poultry. Ladies, this isn't what you want to do any time in your ninth month when labor can kick in at any time. After dinner, we went to the library to research some legal issues relating to mommy's estate. When the library closed, we headed home to get some rest. I got into pajamas and cuddled up to read in bed while Tuvia went to shower.

Suddenly my stomach hurt, but not like a regular stomachache. Noticing that the pains came and went with equal time gaps, I realized I was in the beginning stages of labor. I got dressed, and when Tuvia got out of the shower, I told him it was time to head for the hospital. It was eleven o'clock at night and pouring rain outside. A nervous new father-to-be but the good driver, he ran every red light possible so we would get to the hospital in time. We arrived safely at Tel Hashomer Hospital in Ramat Gan at eleven thirty p.m. I was taken into the prep room, and after being prepped and checked was asked if I needed to use the restroom. I said I did and was helped to it. What happened next was what taught me the lesson about not eating fried foods before labor. Without getting too graphic, all I will say is that I was hit with simultaneous diarrhea and vomiting. Back on the examining table, the midwife checked again and was surprised to see how fast the labor was progressing. That is when she told me "you are doing it the American style." To this day, I have no clue what she was talking about, but I was busy having a baby, and I couldn't care less.

Chanan was born at one thirty in the morning February 13, 1980, healthy and weighing in at 2.970 kg (6 lbs. 6 oz.). Three days later, we went home. Five days later was Chanan's *Brit Milah*, and I woke that morning with a fever. I remember arriving at the last minute feeling awful. Everything went well, and I could get home and get some rest, which I was thankful for, between feedings and diapering.

Chanan was a good baby. He cried little, and I could nap when he slept. When Chanan was born, disposable diapers were not yet in regular use in Israel. I had to use cotton diapers and plastic pants. As most mothers now know, these don't work too well. I remember Tuvia back then as a first-time father; he was afraid to hold Chanan at first, but with some encouragement, he overcame his fear.

When Chanan was four months old, we took him with us on a trip to the United States. He did extremely well on the plane and slept the whole flight. First, we visited with relatives in New York and New Jersey, and then rented a car and traveled to Rhode Island, Washington D.C., Pennsylvania, and flew to Florida and back to New York. We were gone for two months, and by the time we returned home Chanan was six months old and had just stood up and exploring his environment by crawling around.

While in the States, I bought Chanan's first Purim costume—an Indian outfit complete with the feather headband and all. He was so cute. Knowing what I now know I probably would have chosen something else.

In the summer of 1981, a new fast-food restaurant opened in Tel Aviv. The name was Oafalafel, and they made falafel balls from ground chicken. It sounded good, and I wanted to try it, so one evening we went there for dinner. Big mistake. Make that a huge mistake.

After a week, I felt very tired and had no strength to do anything. I never felt that way before, not even in the heat of the summer which I never tolerated well. With a toddler in the house, though, I couldn't afford to stay in bed, so I dragged myself around like a zombie. With no improvement, I went to see my physician. He was puzzled and ran a complete blood count (CBC) to see if he could find what might be the cause making me feel that way. When the results came back, I went to see him. He told me I had a high bilirubin reading and a low hemoglobin reading. He said he didn't understand what was causing havoc to my system and referred me to a specialist for observation.

I saw the specialist once a week. Every time I came, they drew blood. Can you imagine what it's like to get a blood draw every week for one whole year and not have the doctors able to tell you what was wrong? Can you imagine what it was like caring for an active, inquisitive one-year-old baby at the same time?

It was not fun, I tell you. My arms were always sore. I

had to keep track of which arm they used last. Then, just as mysteriously as it came, towards the end of the year the blood test results came back normal. I regained my strength. At that point, all I knew was that I was sick for a year and was on the way to recovery. Still not knowing what I had or what had caused it. I was told, though, to stay away from beans, as it may have been an allergic reaction.

I was not to learn the mystery until years later when I was already in the States, and the Internet was becoming more available in many households, including ours. Surfing the Net I found an allergist that would answer questions free. I wrote to him and told him exactly what had happened and how I was treated. I asked him if he could give a name to what I had.

A short time later, I received a reply from him and finally a diagnosis after about ten years of not knowing. He wrote that a simultaneous high bilirubin and low hemoglobin reading was a sign of serum sickness. He also mentioned that I had been lucky to survive because this condition was often fatal.

The new falafel place where we ate made their falafel balls not only from ground chicken but from added ground Ful beans as well [also known as Fava beans] to the mixture. I was allergic to the beans, which was the first time I'd ever eaten them, and they caused havoc to my system. I was told they belong to the lentil family and to stay away from all beans from that family. The only beans I can safely eat today are Garbanzo beans, which ironically are also within this family but are actually a type of pea and green beans, which are a vegetable and not a true bean.

12
The Lebanon War (1982)

Six days before my twenty-seventh birthday Israeli troops made their way into Lebanon in what would become known as the Lebanon War 1982. We were at home that evening doing nothing in particular. Then the phone rang and Tuvia answered. Minutes later, I said goodbye as he headed off to the base up north until his unit would later join those already in Lebanon. I wasn't scared; it was more of worry that overcame me.

This was my second war in Israel, but this one was different. During the Yom Kippur War, it was mommy and I. I was a teen then. Be it dad or brother, there was no man who left to fight in the war. Now I had a two-year-old toddler to keep safe while my husband left to fulfill his military reserve duty.

I prayed a lot during those days. We spent a lot of time cuddling in bed, just mom and son. It was hard enough to handle the terrible twos in normal conditions, but how does one handle this when it's compounded with a father off fighting a war? To make matters worse, Chanan's invisible friend, the Little Spider, as he called him, showed up and was working overtime, or so it seemed. Anything that went wrong in those days wasn't Murphy's Law at play; the Little Spider caused it all. So now, I was dealing with an innocent toddler and a super active, invisible, sometimes naughty Little Spider. Looking back now, I can laugh at those times. When the Little Spider was up to its shenanigans, it wasn't so funny. It was frustrating.

In the mornings, Chanan attended Ida's playgroup for half a day. She had about eight toddlers all around the age of two. I don't know how she did it, but if you watched them as a group, they looked like little angels. When you spoke to their parents, each of our stories told anything but. We were all sure that Ida had a magic touch. At noon, I picked him up, made lunch for us and when Chanan napped, I slept, too. At night, I listened to the radio, as sleep didn't come anyway. Hoping and praying for the best and fearing the worst, I didn't know exactly where Tuvia was, and with every mention of casualties, my heart skipped a beat.

Writing this and recalling life during the war, I realized that in Israel there are no army wives on bases who support each other while the men are deployed. In Israel, all women with men of service age or reserves age are army wives and we were all in this together. As wives and mothers, we dealt with the family routine: caring for the home, the kids, and sometimes the pets, too. Families shared the same stress, the same fears, and the same basic problems. We were all in the same boat.

On his time off, Tuvia came home to visit with his weapon, an M-16, which we hid on the bedroom porch and locked the door so Chanan couldn't get to it. I don't recall how often he came home to visit, but when he did, the visits were happy quality family time. It was a relief to have him home, and sad and frustrating to have him leave again. It definitely affected my life at the time because every time he left I became a single mom struggling with the ins and outs of daily life. Every time he came home, I became the married mom. The fluctuations in the mom role can be frustrating at times. I'm sure it impacted my son as well though he was only a toddler and understood little at that age, having his dad away and suddenly there again only to leave again must have had some kind of effect on him.

After Tuvia returned home from his duty, we found out that Chanan had a testicular hernia and would need surgery. We bought him a fire engine with a real siren and gave it to him in the hospital. When the siren went off, he told us, "turn it off so it doesn't bother the other kids." That was my son; even at two, he cared about the others. I remember them taking him into the operating room (OR) and we were left to wait in a waiting area that was far from what a waiting room looks like in the States. We stood in a stairwell and waited. Both nervous and worried we were at a loss for words. We stood there silently for a few minutes. Then I noticed tears in my husband's eyes. I tried to comfort him telling him all would be all right. I held him and hugged him. It would have made no sense for both of us to break down. One of us had to be the strong one. I tend to be the stronger one whenever something medical related occurs. When the surgeon was done, and Chanan needed to be taken back to his bed, an aide came out and asked which one of us would carry him back to his bed. Knowing Tuvia wouldn't want to go into the OR, I said I would. The aide told me to take a seat as he would be heavy due to the anesthetic, and once I got my bearing, it would be easier to get up and carry him to the room. I sat there holding him for a while.

He was heavy, and I wasn't sure I could do it. The aide came back in and asked, "Are you ready?" I tried to get up and stand straight but ended up back in the chair. I replied, "I don't think I can do it. He is too heavy for me to carry. I feel very weak for some unknown reason." The aide took Chanan from me, and we walked him back to his bed together. A short time later, I found out I was pregnant with our second child. We were elated. Having just recovered from a medical mystery myself and not planning on getting pregnant so soon, this was a welcome surprise, but as I always say, G-d has his own plans and who are we to question them.

I gave birth to my second son just less than two years since my illness. That would have been bad enough, but to top it off my newborn wasn't holding his weight. At first, I was told he would improve once he settled into a routine nursing schedule, but that didn't happen. After being home for a few weeks and having had quite a few well-baby visits at the Well Baby Center it was clear that something was wrong. Unfortunately, the doctors were striking when he was born, and they were still out of work.

The head nurse at the center, Miriam, had an idea and the courage to take action. She immediately told me to stop nursing Shai and stop mixing milk and water bottles as well. Miriam instructed me to cook rice cereal using only water as the liquid and to make it as thick as possible and feed Shai with that. The cereal was so thick I had to cut the nipples on the bottles large enough for him to eat.

"Weren't you scared to feed such a young infant solid food?"

Many asked me, and you may even wonder the same thing. Shai was only three weeks old, mind you, and yes, I was scared. In fact, I was scared to death, but I had no choice; he had to gain weight to thrive. As his mother, I'd do anything to help him. An end to the doctors' strike was nowhere in sight, and if he lost too much weight we stood the chance of losing him. A mother has to trust someone, so with everything to lose and possibly something to gain, I went ahead with the plan. The first feeding of the thick rice cereal was the hardest. I shook inside praying he wouldn't choke on it. He, on the other hand, just went at it. I could tell he was hungry. Fear didn't let go of me for hours after the feeding until I saw he didn't projectile it up but rather held it down.

For the next two weeks, he either held his weight or gained a tiny bit. Satisfied that we could pull him through until the end of the strike, we continued feeding him in such a manner. About two weeks later, approximately one month after Shai's birth, the doctors' strike ended. Shai was the first baby seen by the Well Baby Center pediatrician on his first day back to work. Though not pleased with his weight, the doctor praised Miriam for her courage in doing the right thing.

He changed Shai over to a soy-based formula besides two cereal bottles a day and observed him over the next few weeks. The soy formula, Isomil, was scarce and hard to find in Israel at the time. We had to special order it from the States by the case through a health food store. As you can imagine, it was a very expensive solution, but we had no choice and could finally convince Kupat Holim, the medical clinic system we belonged to, that it was medically necessary to have this product for Shai and they agreed to reimburse us for the expense. Even if they had continued to refuse to cover the cost, we'd have continued purchasing it, as this was a matter of life and death. The negotiations with the medical clinic to get the approval made me angry. We were talking about a newborn infant here. An infant wasn't supposed to have solid food so early on. The formula would provide the nutrition he needed. Without it, Shai wouldn't thrive, and with it, he gained weight slowly but surely. Shai was then referred to a pediatrician for observation at a local hospital through the first year. Satisfied with the progress Shai had made, this pediatrician put him back on regular milk at one. Today I believe this was the biggest mistake made.

For the first year, before putting him back on regular milk, my son was miserable. He constantly cried and when fed, he'd vomit. He had to be kept in an upright position all the time. Laying him on his back was too dangerous due to the risk of choking on whatever came up and placing him on his stomach would create the effect of a bottle without a cork.

He was either in my hands or in his seat and I was miserable, too, as I felt that I couldn't comfort him enough. Sometimes I felt it was my fault though I knew it wasn't. Caring for him left me drained of energy for my three-year-old, who also suffered because of this. Though he didn't show it, I believe Chanan was jealous of the attention his brother was receiving at the time. I also felt sorry for my neighbors who had to put up with Shai's constant crying, day and night.

For the next six years, he suffered needlessly, though I still had no clue what was causing it. Every time he had milk or anything containing milk, he'd vomit. His pediatrician blamed it on a sensitive stomach and said he'd outgrow it. He didn't. Years later when it led to missed school days I had him examined by an allergist. I figured if his regular physician couldn't figure out what was going on, maybe an allergist could.

We went to see Dr. Jackson in Bellevue, Washington. He tested him for everything including milk. Surprisingly, he didn't show an allergy to milk, but Dr. Jackson had his answer to what must be going on. He told me that it was most likely that Shai was lactose intolerant and that I should try using Lactaid milk instead and see what happened.

After his diagnosis, I kept thinking, why did Shai have to go through all this suffering for nothing. Why have we as parents not been guided to help us deal with this issue? Why had none of the doctors said anything? With Shai's diagnosis, we switched him to Lactaid milk and used Lactaid pills whenever he faced eating dairy products.

For an eight-year-old child, this can be a challenging proposition. There were school parties and birthday parties, most of which served pizza as the food item. At first, it was hard for him to remember that he needed to take a pill, and when he forgot, he was reminded quite quickly by dashing to the bathroom. It took a while but at last, he caught on and from that point on all was normal. Shai even went to summer camp along with his Lactaid pills. He had fun, and he could eat what everyone else ate.

When he was eleven, in order to get it on his medical records officially, we had him tested for lactose intolerance. Of course, he tested positive, and it was finally recorded it in his medical record. With this victory won, I couldn't help thinking whether this could possibly be genetic and part of the medical history I did not know of.

Maybe I was missing something. Could Shai's condition have something to do with my missing link? Could his condition be a genetically transferred one? Being adopted I had no clue. It was then that the urge to find my birth families became intensified. What else was lurking behind the scene that could appear one day and I wouldn't know why? What else was out there that would be important for my children to know, sooner rather than later?

These were pre-Internet days, as we know them today, and I was living in Israel. All that was known to me was that Brooklyn, New York was my birthplace, but not much else. There was no time to wait for the advent of the Internet to bloom. An answer had to be found, but it was almost impossible to succeed. Even so, I searched from Israel, knowing it was a venture into a journey that might have no end. However, also knowing that for my family's sake there was no other option but to pursue it. I had to know it all. My medical information. My heritage. Where I came from. All of that had to be the missing link that would heal the dark black hole within me and find the missing link.

The person who bought our summer home in Carmel,

New York was a lawyer. As my first step, I wrote him a letter seeking advice. He replied that with so little to go on it would be costly, and we might not be able to find anything after all. He advised me not to try, but I just knew I had to, so on and off my search continued. Bumping into brick walls once again, it did not seem like I had a way out.

With nothing much to go on and two small boys who needed me much of the time, I put my search on hold. Without access to other adoptees in search and other sources of advice and help, I wouldn't get far anyway. Though this solution didn't satisfy me, it would have to work for the time being. The only thing I could do at the time was to pray every day that my family would stay healthy.

Gloria Oren

13
Leaving on a Jet Plane

Around 1984, my husband, a mechanical engineer, talked about wanting to work for Boeing in Seattle, Washington for about two years. Coming from New York all I knew was that Washington State was clear across the United States. Nevertheless, this sounded like good news to me. I could hardly believe that he, for whom Israel meant everything, and still does today, was actually considering going to the States. I saw this as my chance to pursue my search actively, and I wasn't going to lose it.

After about fifteen years of living in Israel, going through two wars, and experiencing the premature death of people I had known, I was ready to move on. This time, I'd be doing it with my husband and two young sons. We began preparations and packing things to take with us. The rest of our things we packed for storage at my in-laws while we were gone. Since we could only take eight suitcases with us, there were many decisions to make as to what stayed and what came with us. We had to take clothing, bedding, some basic kitchen items, and the boys' toys and so on.

We were to leave Israel in June 1985. Chanan (John in English), our oldest was five and a half years old and getting ready to enter kindergarten. Shai (Josh in English) was only two years old. This was a good time to make such a move since everything would be new. Chanan would start his elementary school years, and Shai would just be a year away from starting preschool. Between the time of our decision to move and our actual leaving my search stayed on hold. There were too many things to do. There was the packing to do. Selling the apartment, we lived in. Moving our belongings to my in-laws' apartment. Finally, with two young children and eight bags of luggage in tow, we were on our way.

We arrived in New York on June 26, 1985, with no tickets to Seattle, our final destination. The travel agent told us it would be cheaper to get them in the United States. We stayed with mommy's cousin, Clara Turner, in the Bronx for about two weeks. May and Simon, her children, were there, and it was great to be together.

During those two weeks, I suffered from what seemed to me at the beginning of morning sickness. *Could it be?* I said nothing because we had to arrange to get to Seattle. With the Fourth of July travel rush, the earliest available tickets were for July 7. We purchased them. However, since we didn't have a credit card, the agent insisted on using his to reserve a hotel room for one night and a rental car. In the meantime, we visited with relatives and enjoyed our stay.

My relatives couldn't understand what drew us to Seattle. Tuvia didn't have a job lined up with Boeing, just a yearning to work there. However, on July 7, 1985, we boarded the plane bound for Seattle, Washington.

We arrived intact and took the shuttle to the car rental with all eight suitcases. We reserved an economy size car. *What were we thinking when we did that?* I couldn't help but wonder.

When the person at the car rental saw our eight suitcases he said, "There's no way all that will fit in the car." He went back to the office and returned with a key to a Nissan station wagon, upgraded free.

What a neat car! The thing the boys enjoyed most was the "talking lady." If the right door wasn't closed, a female voice would say, "Right door is open." If we forgot to turn off the headlights, she'd warn us, "Lights are on." Chanan couldn't figure out where she was and wanted to know how we could feed her. We all laughed about it years later.

The morning sickness continued, gaining in intensity. We had to rent an apartment since we were briefly staying in a motel. Therefore, we spent the first week driving around the Eastside looking for an apartment in the Crossroads area of Bellevue, Washington. The apartment complex we ended up renting at backed up to a park that would be convenient on nice days with two young boys. It also proved to be helpful in the winter during a snowstorm when we could walk through the park to get to the supermarket to do shopping.

There were a family room, dining nook, kitchen, and a half bathroom downstairs. Upstairs were two bedrooms and a shared bathroom. The boys shared one bedroom, and we had the master bedroom. We set out right away to find a couple of cheap basic items like mattresses to sleep on and a table with four chairs to eat at. Finding both, we began the settling- in process.

We unpacked our belongings and set out to find jobs. I put the boys into daycare part-time so we could go to interviews.

Driving around I noticed a Kinder Care daycare center due to open shortly. There were hiring signs outside the building. Thinking ahead, this seemed to be the perfect arrangement should it turn out that I was indeed pregnant. I went in, applied, and got the job. With one income in hand, though not much, we could get along until Tuvia found a job.

I then made an appointment with an OB-GYN to be tested for pregnancy. What a surprise! Can you believe it! My motherly instincts were right. We would welcome our third child in seven months. Tuvia found a job, though with low pay, but he had to start somewhere. With both of us finding jobs we would have a total of about $24 an hour to start (at least until our third child was born).

I wasn't sure that I could continue working, as it depended on whether there would be space in the infant room by the time I needed it. Working and being forced to speak English on the job, Tuvia was less pressured and felt more at ease.

It wasn't long before February arrived, and on the twentieth, we welcomed our daughter, whom we named Galit. In Hebrew, Galit means "a little wave," like a small bump in the way that was not expected on our arrival in the United States.

The infant room was full where I worked, so I had to leave my job. Left with less money and three small children, it was time to move on, this time to a home of our own where I could also start an in-home daycare. Loving children and having an infant and preschooler at home, I opened my own in-home daycare so I could send Chanan to school in the morning and spend the day with the other two while making money as well.

Looking for a suitable house, we found one not too far from where we were living. It was a split-level with a huge rec room downstairs, which would be perfect for the daycare. The only problem with this location was the struggle to keep it warm during the winter. If I turned up the thermostat so it would be warm enough downstairs, upstairs turned into summer. If the heat were kept to a comfortable temperature, then downstairs it would be cold. We got by with layered clothing downstairs and normal dress upstairs where I served the kids their lunch.

We decided to buy it and moved into the house, and I set up my daycare. Besides my two children, the other young ones I cared for were all part-timers or drop-ins. Chanan enrolled in Camp Fire Girls and Boys, and I met two women who became very good friends, the leader, and the co-leader. The co-leader had a son about Shai's age, and she was looking for daycare arrangements. I now had five children daily with one spot open for drop-ins.

Since we were now settled down and running on a routine, it was time to actively dive into my search for my birth family. I heard about an organization called ALMA on the television and decided to join hoping that my birth mother would also someday join and a match would come about. I didn't make much of this attempt as we still had no computer, and the Internet was still a baby industry. After several years of getting nowhere, I decided not to renew membership with them. I later learned my birth mother had joined ALMA, but the match never came about.

I came down with a cold the next winter, which didn't want

to go away. It turned out to be bronchitis. I was forced to give up my daycare, as I couldn't take the cold temperature downstairs. I was back to the beginning in search of something I could do from home, earn some money, and be with my children.

The end of April 1988 approached and with it the start of the chicken pox season, and though my children had previously avoided coming down with it, this time around Chanan brought it home from school. I thought I was looking at a round of six weeks of chicken pox and that would be that. Well, two weeks later when Chanan was feeling better and back in school, I came down with a severe case of mononucleosis, an infection caused by the Epstein-Barr virus. I was so weak I could barely stand. To top that off, my other two children came down with the chicken pox two days later. I couldn't do anything but lie in bed.

We hired a woman through the Rent-A-Mom agency to care for the kids and prepare my lunch. Chanan complained about her not letting him have snacks when he got home from school because it was before dinner. Knowing she was right but too weak to argue, I called and asked for a replacement. All I wanted at that moment was happy kids. The next day we were sent a younger woman who seemed to be okay but didn't come back the next day. When we received our phone bill in the mail, we noticed that she had placed a call to Paris, France on our phone! Explaining the situation to the phone company, they credited our bill for that call.

Coincidentally, a young Israeli couple was visiting Seattle and looking for something to earn a bit of spending money. A mutual friend put us in contact with them and they came to help. She was wonderful with the kids and an appreciated help to me. We all continued to regain our health. By September, things seemed to be settling down just in time for the couple to continue with their trip. The kids were back in school. We were all healthy, and I could resume my role as mom. I went back to searching for something I could do instead of the daycare.

14
Back to School, Spinning World, and Cancer

In September 1988, I began a course at the Lake Washington Voc-Tech to become a front office Medical Assistant. In November, I experienced dizzy spells. Not the kind where you feel like you're spinning around, but where everything around you is spinning. One minute you're fine and without warning, the walls surrounding you seem to be moving in a whirlwind motion around you. I underwent extensive medical testing for everything under the sun, including Meniere's disease. I had every test you could think of that was available. Doctors tested me for balance, for effects of motions to the head where they actually caused me to go into a vertigo attack, MRIs, and more. From St. Cabrini's Hospital to Swedish Hospital, to the University of Washington Medical Center, I made my rounds of Seattle medical facilities. With the total agreement, the team of doctors made a diagnosis. I had chronic intermittent vertigo.

Thank G-d I was in the States, and the doctors knew what they were looking for. After going through the serum sickness in Israel, where the doctors had no clue as to what was going on, I would be very skeptical if they could diagnose something as complex as this. Why complex? Because dizziness comes in all forms and is a symptom of many, many different conditions, hence the extensive testing to rule out all possibilities.

I began a regimen of a daily dose of Meclizine to control vertigo, and thankfully, it both agreed with me and worked. I've been taking it ever since, and should I forget to take it before going to bed, I will know in the morning, no need for reminders. Take it or deal with a vertigo attack. Many times over the years, my doctors have asked me to try to stop using it and see what happens. I tell them I don't think it is necessary as when I rarely forget to take it at night, I wake up with an attack. They've agreed with me, that daily use is what keeps me going. That's not to say that I never get an attack even with the medication; I do, but it is predictable. I tend to get them when I have bad congestion from a cold, which is why at the first sign of a cold I try to fight back with saline nasal spray to keep the passages open, hoping to prevent an attack. Sometimes it works, sometimes it doesn't. Despite this situation, missed class time, and all, I wrote a research paper on Tay-Sachs disease and graduated from the class, with the support of my teacher, Mrs. Vered Tolaroy.

The school promised its students jobs, but the reality was that most of us weren't able to find one by the end of the course. Out of nineteen students, only three were successful in gaining employment. However, it was the best thing I have done and money well spent.

So, with no promised jobs on the horizon, I looked around for other options and decided to try a home-based travel agency. Had I known it would be a very competitive industry and almost impossible to break into, I would have looked for something else. I did that for a while but wasn't getting anywhere. The industry was about to cut commissions so it was time to move on.

Alas, this wasn't the end to my medical problems. Sometime between 1988 and 1990, I developed a mitral valve prolapse, which meant, at the time, that I'd have to take antibiotics before every dental visit, and/or other surgical procedure to prevent germs from getting into my blood system during the procedure being done. Can you imagine taking four Amoxicillin pills, driving to the dentist, being given numbing medication, having whatever necessary procedure was done, and then driving home? Scary? Yes, but I had no choice. I even gave it a name—my zombie dental days.

Then in 1990, Tuvia lost his job and was unemployed for quite a few months. The market didn't look promising, and jobs were scarce. Shortly before his being laid off, we had just moved into our new house. We had to start dipping into our savings, never a good thing. I knew I had to help out, and though other jobs were scarce, jobs in the healthcare arena were plentiful. I updated my resume and began submitting it. Without knowing it, this choice later turned out to be a lifesaver.

I applied for a job with Check Medical, a walk-in clinic, later known as Health Sound Clinics and now as US Healthworks. Acing the interview, there were only two things left to do before I could start to work, the drug testing and the pre-employment physical. During the pre-employment physical, the doctor noticed my glands were swollen. She asked, "Have you had a cold recently?"

I replied, "I did, about five weeks earlier. But I just saw my doctor a week ago, and he said all was fine."

"Did you know that your glands are swollen?"

I said, "No, I didn't."

I think she noticed more but didn't want to say anything then. She at once stopped the exam. "Well go see your physician, as soon as possible, and let me know when you're feeling better. We'll reschedule the exam. Meanwhile, I'll wait for the result of the drug testing."

I went home, called my doctor's office, and scheduled an appointment for the same day.

I went to see my physician, Dr. W who referred me to an ENT (ear, nose, and throat) specialist. "Schedule an appointment within the next week, from the waiting room, and let my medical assistant know when that would be."

I did that and headed home. By the time, I walked into the house there was a message waiting for me from the ENT's office. I was to call at once to reschedule the appointment.

I called.

"Your doctor called saying he wants you to be seen tomorrow so we have to reschedule your appointment accordingly."

I rescheduled the appointment and tried not to think of the urgency that evolved.

Dr. A, the ENT specialist, examined me and said "I'm not quite sure what it is, but it might be worse than it appears. Let's get you set up for a neck biopsy tomorrow."

The neck biopsy was scheduled for the next morning in the lab at Overlake Hospital.

"I'll call as soon as the results are in."

I don't wish this type of biopsy on my worst enemy. I arrived at the lab as scared as could be. The lab technician, a tall, broad-shouldered guy, brought out this huge suction needle. Just seeing it could cause someone to faint. Now I was super scared.

"I'm going to insert the needle into the growth in your neck and suction out some of the content to examine it so we can determine if the mass is benign or malignant," he said. "I need you to be as still as you can. I don't want to hurt you."

He used only local anesthetic, but as scared as I was, I felt it all. He started poking me with the needle, and every time he went in, tears ran down my cheeks. He didn't get a sample.

"Please stop. It hurts too much," I kept begging him.

At last, after about five tries, he gave up and sent me back to the ENT.

Dr. A set up a date for a surgical biopsy under general anesthesia for a few days later. From there things moved very quickly. Within two weeks, I had the biopsy as well as an additional probing surgery, which included the removal of my spleen, which was the size of a grapefruit. I was diagnosed with Hodgkin's disease, the nodular sclerosing lymphoma type. My doctor classified it as stage 2 meaning there was a mass in my neck and signs of a small one developing near the lung.

I underwent three months of radiation therapy and was told that most likely in the fifth year after this therapy I'd have the onset of thyroid failure. Well, you missed that one, doc; I got lucky there, and it occurred during my sixth year of remission.

Meanwhile from 1988 to 1996, the Internet continued to develop. Having time during recuperations from all the above mentioned, my skill of getting around online also improved. I discovered many new resources, some of which proved quite helpful, in my search once I resumed it actively. I created a list of sites I wanted to visit in detail, groups I wanted to watch and consider joining, and so on. First, I'd let my body heal; then I'd put my mind to work.

During this time, I also went through lots of pain and soul searching. I had lots of time to think, and I decided that no matter what, I must try to find my birth family. Had I not taken the class and not leaned back on it, and had it not been for the observant Check Medical doctor, I most likely wouldn't be here today, as there were no noticeable symptoms at all. Whether it was a coincidence or someone watching over me from above, I knew that overcoming any type of cancer was the second chance at life. I also knew that if I was going to restart my search actively, now was the time to do so. So onward ho—my search went into action once again.

In April 1999, it became difficult to eat. Every swallow hurt and caused coughing bouts that were choking at the least. I went to see a gastroenterologist who diagnosed a narrowing of the esophageal tube and ordered an endoscopy. A date was set. By now, I was no longer afraid of medical procedures; hey, I think I've been through enough of them to convince me that all would be well. The gastroenterologist sprayed my throat with a sedating medication and then inserted a thin tube with a balloon at the end. Once in place, he inflated the balloon to widen the esophageal tube. Everything went well though the doctor warned me that this might reoccur.

In May 2000, I went in for an annual physical with my radiology oncologist. He didn't like the way an old mole, sitting right smack in the middle of the 1990 incision, looked. He advised me to have my dermatologist look at it and make the final decision, but as far as he was concerned, it had to be removed. A few weeks later, I had a consultation with my dermatologist and as soon as he saw it, he said it was coming out. I scheduled an appointment, and in July 2000, I had it removed. I don't know what was worse—the local anesthetic injection or the horrific itching the first two days after the surgical procedure. All I know is that I was in tears almost the whole time or constantly reading. By the end of the second day, I was ready to walk on the ceiling. I must have read more Harlequin books in those two days than I've read in my entire life. Hmm…*wonder why I chose Harlequin.* That's how bad the itching was, and no one had warned me that it would itch so bad. It seemed like I'd never get the pathology report back from the lab, but two months later (why it took so long I did not understand) it came back—benign—thank G-d. I was elated.

Exactly three years later, as my gastroenterologist had warned on the first occurrence, in April 2002, my esophageal tube closed up again to 9 cm and a repeat endoscopy was scheduled. This time, the doctor opened it to 18 cm, and it hasn't closed up again since. I am on his list for repeat endoscopies every five years, though, just to make sure all is well and there is no scarring because of previous procedures, or any new developments. The last one in 2014, (two years overdue) showed all to be well.

15
My Search Adventures

With the arrival of the Internet, still in its developing stages but mature enough to begin searching around in 1994, I could search online. It would open up the doors not previously available. Venturing out into no-man's-land online I first had to familiarize myself with what was then available; not as much as today. I found The Adoptees Mailing List and began reading some of the posts. I continued reading the posts for several days, and then started commenting on some of them. My goal was to become known among the members. Then I started posting messages as well. People started responding. Surprisingly, I learned that I wasn't the only one born in Brooklyn who never had an amended birth certificate. I realized that it was a common thing for that period in Brooklyn hospitals, not only at Beth-El Hospital where I was born.

Through this list, I met other adoptees for the first time in my life. It was a wake-up call. There were other adoptees like me, who had experienced the veil of secrecy while growing up. I had never before met other adoptees so realizing that I wasn't the only adult adoptee in the world was huge. Suddenly, it felt like I had friends who understood where I was coming from. The anger that built up over the years. The black hole created by all the unknowns. The secrecy all started coming together. We were all similar circumstances. I had someone to talk to, someone who I could relate to, and someone who in return could relate to me.

I met people from Brooklyn and other New York areas, from Montreal and Nova Scotia, Canada and other places. People from these areas became my shoulders to lean on for specific inquiries. The others provided helpful general informational feedback in response to questions such as "What do I do next?", "How do I locate such-and-such?" and so on. Some of us developed close friendships, and we eventually found ourselves sending email messages to each other.

Continuing my journey, I came across other helpful sites. Having read everything my hands could get a hold of related to adoption searches and reunions, I was a sponge that couldn't get enough. Over a period of eight years, devouring as much as I could read, everything from articles online to postings on lists, and even books, which is not to say I hadn't been reading about adoption searches since 1980. I had, and in total that would make my search time equal sixteen years. I watched movies about adoptees, some of which told the stories of reunion. Every one of them brought on the flow of tears. *When will my turn come? Will I ever know who I truly am?*

We decided that the kids were old enough to enjoy Disneyland, so we took a trip to Los Angeles. Besides giving the kids a fun vacation, I had another important goal to accomplish on this trip. I knew that Rabbi Twersky, a dear, close friend of my adoptive parents, was then living in Los Angeles. Who better than he would know other rabbis in the areas where he previously lived?

Let me explain. Rabbi Twersky and my adoptive parents came from the same town in Bessarabia. Perhaps he held the key to a lead for information about my adoption. Little did I know how instrumental a role he played in my adoption. In fact, for several years, his daughter and I corresponded as pen pals and became quite good friends without me actually knowing how close I was to the information I needed during all those years.

I called Rabbi Twersky and asked if my husband and I could visit with him as I wanted to discuss something with him. He welcomed us, and we headed out to his home. I learned from him that he thought my birth mother's family was from Nova Scotia, Canada, and that her father had a paper mill. Wow! Not knowing at the time that the paper mill issue was quite farfetched, I researched Jewish paper mill owners in Nova Scotia. Of course, I didn't get very far with that either, as there weren't any or, at least, any I could find.

I also took this information and wrote to the Atlantic Jewish Council (AJC) in Halifax, Nova Scotia, Canada seeking help or advice as to how I could find her. I identified myself as my mother's friend, which was necessary, because if I said I was an adoptee seeking my birth mother I might not have even received an attempt to help. People feared to get involved in issues involving sealed records, or they feared that it might be someone they knew and didn't want to get involved. Positioning myself as an outsider, a friend, they responded with warmth and sent me a directory of all the Jewish institutions in the Halifax, Nova Scotia area. They also said they published a monthly newsletter for their members and offered to put a blurb in for me at no charge. Unfortunately, this offer had no results at all.

I contacted other leads I came across and even the local Jewish newspaper. I was going to send the paper a short article but never got around to it, and in the end, glad I didn't.

By 1995 after not getting close to finding what I sought, I mustered up the courage and wrote my cousin Elisa a long, heartfelt letter. She followed up by calling my Aunt Ruth, her mother, to see if she recalled any of the information I had obtained from the rabbi. She acknowledged that my birth mother was a teenager at the time and that she was Jewish. She said she remembered her name was Marcia, but couldn't recall a surname. She also said I looked a lot like her from what she remembered.

Aunt Ruth added that when my birth mother entered the hospital to give birth to me, she or the hospital staff used my adoptive mother's name on the records. I later found out this was a common practice in the hospital labor wards in New York during the 1950s. Both Aunt Ruth and Aunt Mildred visited her in the hospital and met my grandmother. Aunt Ruth added that when I was brought home my adoptive parents didn't even have a crib yet so they placed me in a padded dresser drawer. Aunt Ruth acknowledged that Marcia was from Canada but wasn't sure about Nova Scotia, though. She thought it was more likely that she was from Montreal.

Great! My search route now took on a V-shaped road, one branch leading to Montreal and the other to Nova Scotia.

Decisions, decisions, decisions! Which way do I go? Was the rabbi right or was my aunt right? Would I find my treasures in Montreal or in Nova Scotia? My search went on.

When my cousin Jay heard that I was actively searching for my birth mother, he offered to help out with researching the Nova Scotia possibility for that branch. He said he was going to contact the Census Bureau in Halifax to try to track down how many Jewish women and girls there were in Nova Scotia between the years 1939 and the late 1950s. I guess he wasn't able to find this information as I never heard back from him with a number.

However, a few days later Jay called to say he located two synagogues in Nova Scotia. He spoke to one rabbi, whose son worked for the Jewish Historical Society of Nova Scotia, and who gave Jay his son's telephone number. Jay spoke with him, and he promised to research it further. He did inform Jay that all the mills were found either in Pictou or Richmond Counties. Jay also spoke to someone in a Canadian newsgroup, and that person was checking out something for Jay as well. Jay asked if he could call Rabbi Twersky and my pediatrician. Not sure exactly what his reason was for this, but I gave him the go ahead.

At the same time, I was beginning to feel more comfortable online. I continued corresponding with people in the United States and Canada, now mainly concentrating on those in Montreal and Nova Scotia. They were all kind and tried to help, but I kept running into brick wall dead ends. I was reading *Torn from the Heart* by Louise Jurgens, a birth mother who had found her daughter. It was a great book that led me to think the following: if my birth mother was searching for me as well, would she be able to find me having moved around so much? This had not occurred to me before reading this book. I realized it might be harder and likely dependent on how far she would go to obtain such information. I knew two things, though: one was that wherever I was, there would likely be some sort of paper trail that could be traced; and two, if our finding each other was meant to be, it would happen. The author's address was given at the back, so I wrote her a letter. We continued sending letters for a while relating our stories to each other.

I began to wonder whether all this searching would ever bear any fruit; yet, all along, I had a feeling that the time put into my search wasn't going to waste. I felt in my heart, that someday, somewhere, we would meet again. However, I didn't want to set myself up for a broken heart. I chose to keep this feeling to myself rather than share it with anyone. That way, if I was wrong, no one could tell me "Told you so," or something like that. I had an eerie feeling of certainty that it would come to be. We would meet again eventually; my gut feeling told me so. How and when? I had no idea.

From the many books and postings of successful searches ending in despair, I knew that I must be prepared. This I did by telling myself over and over again that even the worst news was better than not knowing at all, and went on with my search.

During my search, many events occurred. I encountered an

eighty-year-old woman who began corresponding with me. In mid-February, she surprised me with a Valentine's Day card in the mail, my first ever outside the ones we exchanged in school as kids. She wished me luck in my search. A total stranger sending me a card. I received other notes in the mail wishing me luck as well as many email messages, all from total strangers.

On the other hand, I did encounter one nasty incident along the way. I was given a lead from a rabbi in Montreal and followed up on it. After chatting with the man for a few minutes, I realized there was a mistake. I excused myself, saying I was sorry to have bothered him and hung up. I made a note of the fact that this lead led to nowhere and continued. A few minutes later he called back threatening to have me arrested for harassment. You read that right. Harassment! What nerve! I know it isn't every day that someone calls to inquire if your sister ever spent time in New York while she was pregnant as a teenager and had given birth to a daughter that she had given up for adoption. But give me a break—harassment—one simple five-minute phone call in my book doesn't qualify as harassment. Had I consistently called him and bugged him to say his sister was the one I was searching for I could understand, but not from one measly call. Anyway, that was a good scare but persistence took the lead, and my search went on.

One day I came across some information that led me on a very interesting detour. I was once again researching the mills when I discovered a possible lead, a paper mill owned by two

Irish Jewish brothers. Researching this deeper I discovered several articles from various publications. One of the articles talked about the castle they owned in Ireland. Can you feel my gears churning? *Wow! Could it be that this was my ancestry? Castle owners in Ireland who also owned their own plane?* It's nice to think big and I couldn't stop thinking about this until I reached another article that mentioned that they both had only sons. Darn! It was, like many other things, too good to be true. On to the next lead I went.

I continued searching only to keep bumping into more brick walls than leads to follow-up on. During the last six years of my search, I managed to locate the parents of one good childhood friend and through them I reconnected with her. I wrote them to inquire if they remembered anything from the period of my birth, as they were neighbors in the same building. After some phone calling, Helen got back to me with news that she had the name of the girl whom she thought wrote that famous note back when I was four years old. She had lived one floor above us. I never did contact her to inquire as to why she wrote that note in the first place, and perhaps that's a good thing. Frankly, from other things I've learned along the way it didn't seem to work age wise. However, the problem is that no one I know of that building and am still in contact with today can remember any other teens or older tweens who lived there at the time. I guess it's no longer important to know why the mysterious note writer did it. Instead, I would like to one day locate whoever it was and send a thank you note. After all, had it not been for that note, I most likely would never have known I was adopted.

One night in April 1996, I had a dream. Let me tell you, I don't have dreams too often but when I do they are as strange as can be. This one was no different. As I slept and entered the dream stage, an image, and a voice appeared in the distance. It was a female image with a feminine voice. I couldn't tell if it was a young woman or an older one, but I distinctly heard her call out to me saying "Gloria" repetitively. I tried to determine who this was, what she looked like, and so on; instead I found myself sitting up in bed, my whole body shaking, and the image and voice were gone. *Who could she have been? What message was she trying to deliver? Why did she appear in the first place?* Questions seemed to pop up every few seconds, and I could not stop wondering.

"Are you okay?" Tuvia asked me. He wasn't used to me waking like this so suddenly during the night.

"I had a dream," I said, "and saw a female image calling out to me from afar."

"Who was it?"

"I don't know. I couldn't tell and now it's all gone. That's what is bugging me."

I lay awake trying to figure it out for the rest of the night. By morning, I still hadn't come up with a clue. Throughout the next day, it wouldn't leave my mind. Sort of like, when a character takes hold of your muse and won't let go. *Was it Hannah, my adoptive mother, trying to tell me something? Was it my birth mother or grandmother warning that the time we meet is coming closer? Was it someone else, and if so, who?* It drove me nuts not to be able to decipher what the dream was about and understand what was going on. With time, it faded and let me be.

16
Gift of a Lifetime

One morning in June 1996, precisely eight days before my forty-first birthday, something unexpected took place that was about to change my life forever. My father-in-law called at six thirty a.m. from Israel. This was quite unusual since Tuvia left for work earlier than that, and his dad always called when Tuvia was home. *Why was he calling so early?* Well, speaking with him gave me my answer.

He was calling me, not Tuvia. Someone named Yehudah called him from Jerusalem wanting my address and phone number. My father-in-law wanted to know if he should give out the information. Since caution is the word today when asked for personal information, I said "no." *Why would I give my address and phone number to some Yehudah guy from Jerusalem when I had no idea who he was?* I asked if the person left his phone number. Since he did, I got the number and proceeded to call. I felt it was safer for me to get his phone number and for me to call him. Looking back on this logic I'm not so sure. Would it matter who called first if he were a bad guy with some fraudulent scheme? I don't think so, but for some unknown reason, it seemed the right thing to do at that time.

I was surprised to get a young child on the phone. I asked to speak with the father. I was told that he just went out for a minute, and if I left my number he would call me right back.

Within five minutes he called back introducing himself as

Yehudah. I asked him what he wanted from me and this was his reply:

"Are you sitting down?"

"No, why? Should I be sitting?"

"Yes, please sit down as what I'm about to tell you will be long awaited news," he continued. "My wife's cousin is your birth mother."

Did I hear that right? Did he just say his wife was my birth mother's cousin? Was this really happening? It was like a dream. All sensations of hot and cold occurred at the same time. Goosebumps crept up my arms. I wasn't sure I'd heard him correctly so I asked him to repeat what he just said, and he did. I knew he was serious. *Why would anyone seek me out through my father-in-law and call the U.S. from Israel if he wasn't?* I spoke with Yehudah for about fifteen minutes and asked how he reached my father-in-law. Yehudah explained that he had an acquaintance who worked at the U.S. Embassy in Tel Aviv, and he had contacted this person to inquire how to go about finding me. Since we were American citizens when my mother and I lived in Israel upon her death, an American death certificate was also filed and a copy had remained with the embassy. On it, I was listed as an heir. They also found information that I had married in Israel. To find the family name and the names of witnesses on the marriage certificate who may be able to help he had to contact the Rabbinate. Yehudah seems to have the right connections everywhere, so he now went to another acquaintance who worked there and asked for help. Since my father-in-law was one of the witness signers Yehudah contacted him. I thanked him for all he had done and hung up.

I was floating on cloud nine. Make that higher than cloud nine.

Remember that dream about a woman who was calling my name, standing off at a distance; *Maybe, I was missing something.* I couldn't tell clearly whether the image looked like someone I knew or not. *Could the dream I had a month before have been a sign that my search was drawing near its end? Could Shai's condition have something to do with my missing link? Could his condition be a genetically transferred one?* Being adopted I had no clue. It was then that the urge to find my birth families intensified once again. What else was lurking behind the scene that could appear one day and I wouldn't know why? What else was out there that would be important for my children to know, sooner rather than later?

And now this. Incredible! Suddenly it seemed as if my birth mother had found me and was calling out to me. After searching for all those years, seeking information from sources in New York, Montreal, and Nova Scotia, all it took, in the end, was one phone call, and of all places, from Jerusalem, Israel.

First, I called Tuvia at work to tell him the great news. Acting as chair of the Social Concerns Committee at Galit's school that year, I had scheduled a meeting that morning and had to be there on time. *Could I do it? Could I manage to make the call I dreamed of making for a very long time, get Galit ready, and still arrive on time?* I had to. I had no other choice. I'd waited long enough and now that it was finally all coming together as wished, I had to take my chances. I had to place this very important call.

Then I went to wake up my daughter, Galit and get her ready for school. I woke her up by whispering in her ear "You now have a real grandmother." As I said that, goose bumps once again crept up along my arms. I could hardly believe it myself, as it had not had time to fully sink in. Since Galit was only nine months old when her paternal grandmother passed away and never had the chance to meet my mother, who had passed away years before she was born, this was a big event for her. It was also her dream. She had yearned to have a grandmother like all her friends, and I hoped in my heart that I could one day give it to her. Now that this became reality, it was another reason I wanted to make that call as soon as possible.

She was up, dressed, ate breakfast, and ready to call her biological grandmother in no time. I dialed with trembling fingers, the ringing began, and then she answered. My heart skipped a beat or two and I said hello. I told her she wasn't going to believe this but I was her long lost daughter that she had made an adoption plan for in 1955.

After a pause, I told her that her cousin's husband, Yehudah, had called me earlier that morning. Though I thought a call out of the clear blue sky would shock her, I had no idea that in the time it took to get Galit ready and place the call, Yehudah would have already called her to say I'd be calling soon. Though both sides were happy, the quickness that all this took place demanded some time to absorb everything so we exchanged contact information. Galit spoke with her grandmother for a few minutes, and we said goodbye. That was the start of a very successful reunion. Later when I asked her what it felt like to hear my voice on the phone after a period of almost forty-one years, she said, "It felt like fireworks going off under my seat. It was the greatest feeling in the world."

We started corresponding by e-mail and many interesting bits of information were passed in both directions. Through this communication, I found out that my birth mother had suffered and survived thyroid cancer in 1976 and was now a Type-2 diabetic. In a message I sent my birth mother on June 5, 1996, one day after making contact with her, I wrote:

"We have found each other and a new chapter in life is about to begin. In Hebrew, there is a saying . . . Yesh Elohim Bashamaim—[there is a G-d in the heavens]. G-d was watching over both of us, letting us both survive cancer because we were destined to meet again. This reunion is G-d's will, and I will not let it go to pieces. We have waited too long to find each other, and now must get on with our lives together.... it is Elohim (G-d) that makes miracles happen."

On that same day, I called my biological maternal grandmother and spoke with her for the very first time in my life. I had goosebumps creep up my arms throughout the conversation. I had never in my farthest dreams thought I'd ever get to speak with my grandmother, especially not when I was just about to turn forty-one. My grandmother told me that Hannah, my mother, had called her years before and told her we might move to Israel sometime in the future. It's funny and ironic how things sometimes come together in reality. Here she told my grandmother we might move to Israel, and when I was fourteen, I requested to spend a year there. Had she planned it all along?

She had also given her the store's phone number, which my grandmother had written on a small piece of paper, which she saved all these years. When we met she gave it to me as proof that they had contact with my adoptive parents. By the way, Rabbi Twersky had told me when we visited him that my birth mother's family had corresponded with my adoptive parents for the first few years and then stopped.

In a response to me on June 5, 1996, my birth mother wrote regarding what she would have named me had she been able to keep me.

She wrote, "My choice was Elizabeth after Elizabeth Taylor…she was my favorite actress since National Velvet, and she was so beautiful as I hoped you would turn out to be…"

Wow! Just think, even then I was compared to a movie star!

On June 10, 1996, Mom wrote, "It seems everything happens fast or not at all. Your whole life changes in a minute. One day I have one grandchild and now I have four—wow! Like the instant birth of quads! One day I have two children, now I have three. My head is spinning, and I haven't landed yet."

On June 11, I replied to Mom's last e-mail. One of the things I wrote was, "For once in forty-one years I am a completed puzzle, a whole person, and for the first time in many months

I am sleeping well at night and not getting up tired." I ended with the following birthday thank you:

"Just wanted you to know
On my very special day
I'm sending hugs and kisses
So they can help me say . . .
Thank you for my birthday!"

The next day was my birthday, and though I was turning forty-one, it was the first birthday I shared with my mom in as many years. I sent her a daughter's birthday thought in an e-mail as follows:

"There is a great big wish I'm sending
From me to you today
It is full of happy thoughts and dreams
That are sure to help me say
Though I can't be with you
Each and every day
I think of you with every breath
In a very special way."

The first card I received from mom would be followed by much more. Mom made it on her computer, herself, and it said,

[Outside] I am proud of you, Gloria

"A daughter adds beauty, joy, and love to life"

[Inside] No words can describe the pride, and the gratitude, too,

That comes from having a daughter to love and to cherish—like you.

Happy Birthday With Love

[Mom's signature followed by—the first of many, I hope, Mother]

I still have it in my correspondence binder where it has been since the day I received it. I also received a card from my grandmother and I was in tears of joy. It was so beautiful, but what touched me most was what she had written, "There's so much explaining to do on my part, and I do hope you will forgive me!"

Of course, I forgave her, though I don't know exactly for what, as I never had any harsh feelings toward her nor toward my mom. In fact, I had never considered the possibility of ever finding my grandmother as well, even if I did find my mom. How could I? I was placed in the hands of a loving family and had everything I needed.

Like a jigsaw puzzle whose four sides had to close completely to be a completed whole, so was I. With three sides of the completed whole closed the only missing link left to be found was my birth father. I had already met my birth mother, birth grandmother, and maternal birth siblings. Now, at least, I had a name to relate to, and that, in and of itself, was a closure. But with a name I now also had a new journey to venture about in, the journey of discovering my paternal ancestral history.

On June 15, 1996, Mom sent me an e-mail informing me of my birth father's death. She hadn't been told, and when she tried reaching him where he had worked, they gave her the sad news. My birth father was only fifty when he died of cancer of the esophagus. As I had said before I was prepared to find both good and bad news, so learning of my birth father's death was sad but not shocking; much wanted and needed.

On June 17 I e-mailed Mom and one of the things I enclosed was a quote by Ralph Waldo Emerson—"For everything you have missed you have gained somcthing."

I wrote about how when I think back to how I found out I was adopted I wonder if that foolish one had not written that note and left it so that I would find it...would I ever have been told the truth? Though it wasn't the most pleasant of notes one could find, I am somewhat thankful to the mysterious one for at least telling me that information.

As I stated at the beginning, the fact that I was adopted had been a family secret, and no one ever dared speak about it or anything related to it. Moreover, no one ever mentioned that my parent's first child was also adopted. I wasn't even sure my family knew about my adoption until I approached my closest cousin, and it turned out that they knew all along but never mentioned it. Surprisingly, some of my cousins didn't know. The main thing is we have found each other, and we're once again together.

Now, don't get me wrong here, I adored my parents and had all that I needed, but the umbrella of secrecy kept my biological heritage from me. And that buildup over the years eventually led to an inner anger, familiar to many adoptees, especially as I began to understand things more and my questions, for the most part, went unanswered. Yes, I've missed my Mom, in my growing years, but I've gained her back young enough to still enjoy a good number of years together. Thanks to you,

Gloria Oren

I've learned about both my maternal roots and my especially interesting paternal heritage and history.

17
Reunion

On July 2, 1996, a few weeks after the first contact with my birth mother, my family boarded a plane for Toronto, Ontario. My birth mother and half-sister were living in Bolton, a suburb of Toronto. My husband and oldest son only had one week to spend with us, due to work and summer school commitments. I had my ticket as well as my other two children's tickets set up for a possible extension at a minimal charge.

My birth mother, half-sister, and my niece met us at the airport with excitement and lots of embraces. We were both happy and cautious at the same time. It was surreal. At that moment, neither my birth mother nor I shed tears of any kind. The tears were to come later when we were together and out of sight of the others.

My birth mother had rented a van so we could all get to her home. Her friend had come along to take pictures. We spent one day at my birth mother's home where I was able to spend time with her and my half-sister, Rachel Lynn. My daughter had time to get to know her first cousin, Amanda. We stayed up until the wee hours of the morning talking, looking at pictures and so on. I was amazed to learn that my oldest son, Chanan, shared his name not only with my adoptive mother but with my maternal great grandfather. The tears started flowing as we spoke of how it all had taken place years ago, and how amazingly we crossed paths once again, this time, never to be parted again.

It was wonderful to be together. We were both still floating on Cloud Nine.

The four generations of women – July 1996

On the fourth, all seven of us boarded a plane headed for Nova Scotia to meet the rest of the family. My niece was spending ten days at a drama camp so she didn't join us on this trip. In Nova Scotia, we met my two aunts, their families, my half-brother and his wife whom he later would divorce, and most of all, my grandmother, Aida Fritz, whom everyone referred to as Bubbie. This was exciting for me as I had said before I never thought, in my farthest dreams, that I would be so fortunate to meet my grandmother after so many years. Bubbie hadn't been feeling well the past few years, so she told me then, "I'm ready to go now." She passed away shortly after.

Unknown to any of us was the surprise awaiting us. Remember Yehudah? Well, Yehudah and his family were there too. They were on a summer vacation trip to visit with their families further down the Annapolis Valley. When they heard we were arriving that same day, they decided to stop at my aunt's house where the reunion was taking place.

Yehudah has an interesting story in and of itself. He was born to a non-Jewish family in the Annapolis valley area of Nova Scotia, but after marrying Maureen Naomi Fritz, my birth mother's cousin, he converted and became an Orthodox Jew. They later moved and settled in Jerusalem, Israel. That was an extra nice surprise since none of this would have been taking place if not for Yehudah's generous help in making it happen by tracking me down. We spent two exhausting days with the family, during which we were taken to the family business then operated by my aunt and her husband, as well as the residences where my birth mother grew up. We then flew back to Toronto.

My husband and oldest son were to leave the next day, so when we landed in Toronto; we headed to the airline counter to extend the rest of our tickets for another two weeks. It was the time we needed; besides, my Mom, which is now how I thought of her, was to undergo minor knee surgery, and I wanted to be there for her. During the day of the surgery, my half-sister watched the girls, and I went with Mom to the hospital. It was an outpatient surgery, but someone had to drive her home, so I did.

The time spent with Mom during those two weeks shed

light on the other side of my heritage. From Mom, I learned who my birth father was. She related to me that they were exactly one year apart in age; therefore, they had been through school together. Sadly, two weeks ended too fast. We parted vowing never to be separated again and to stay in contact.

Over the next four years, I had also made contact with my birth father's family and we began corresponding by e-mail. About two months after my return from Toronto, not having anything special to do, I decided to research the Longley surname in Nova Scotia in the hope of finding someone in my birth father's family. I sent an e-mail to all those matching the surname Longley that I could find in Canada. It didn't take too long before I had a possible lead. After some initial questions based on information I had been given by Mom, this contact turned out to be my half-brother. From that point on e-mail and additional contacts were made. After forty years I went from being an only child to one of a total of ten children, nine living, and too many relatives to count.

My birth father passed away over eight years before our reunion. My birth father, unlike my birth mother, was not Jewish but had once told her that he would convert if only her father would accept him. She knew that was not going to happen. But he was from a huge notable family that played a large part in the settlement of the American colonies many years ago as well as holding many different high-level positions in Canada.

One of the first families to settle in Groton, Massachusetts, was William Longley and Joanna Goffe, my eighth great-grandparents. They emigrated from England to colonial America and belonged to the Puritan movement. Later when John Longley, "the Captive," married Sarah Prescott (my seventh great grandparents) the family gained yet another person of fame, her nephew, Colonel William Prescott, of the Battle of Bunker Hill, the first battle of the Revolutionary War. Col. William Prescott was my first cousin seven times removed, and his father Benjamin was my sixth great granduncle.

This information interested me, and my love of genealogy research blossomed. There are many others of this time period within my ancestry who played roles in the growth of our country, and I'm proud of them all. Others researching the family have made claims that there is a connection to John Adams and John Quincy Adams as well. I have yet to find the exact connection, but there are a few Adams found on the line so I may yet find it one day.

My birth father was married twice and I have been in contact with his second wife and my three half-brothers from that marriage. When I began corresponding with his second wife after connecting with my half-brother, she was concerned about me and my father's other children from both of his marriages. From my e-mail messages, she was of the opinion that people's doubts and callous remarks would hurt me unless I was an extremely unfeeling person. I wrote back to her that I was a very feeling person, and that I have experienced callous remarks in the past. I don't think she fully agreed with me, but we are still in touch with each other.

Growing up in Brooklyn, New York in a Jewish neighborhood that turned mostly black, there was much prejudice and a lot of anti-Semitism. I heard many remarks against me in the past. I went to schools in neighborhoods where there were times we could not play in the yard at recess because the high school teens on the other side of the fence would start fighting with us and calling us all kinds of things. These teens were both black and white. It was not a matter of color, rather a much deeper issue. They even stole our bus passes, and one day they stole mine, too. I had to go home with the principal until my mother could pick me up because I had no money for the bus home. I knew what mean people were like. I've lived through that experience several times during my childhood.

Anyway, my relationship with my birth father's second wife grew stronger as our correspondence developed, and she later asked me to consider her as my stepmother, which I was honored to do.

I have met a half-sister from our father's first marriage. We have been e-mailing each other for years now, and I've spoken to her on the phone several times. On a family trip to Calgary, Alberta where we joined up with my mom, half-sister, and my niece, I got to meet my paternal half-sister as well. She is a nurse, is married and has four boys, among them a set of twins. I have since discovered that twins were in abundance in my paternal history. In fact, there were even triplets, too. Though these multiple births escaped me, there is a chance that somewhere along the line, more sets of multiple births might occur; I have warned my daughter.

I've made contact with and met a paternal first cousin living in British Columbia, and our daughters have become very close cousins.

I've made contact with my other paternal half-sister through Facebook and have put together a Facebook page for the family line stemming from Groton, Massachusetts. Within a short time membership grew and suddenly there were forty-two of us, some of whom I have never heard of. I discovered a third cousin and third cousin once removed, as well as several seventh cousins and some fifth and sixth cousins. I continue finding new relatives all the time and have recently made contact with a fifth cousin living in California.

There is nothing like feeling whole, and genealogy helps this wholeness continue. I continue learning about my heritage through genealogy research. It provides a vast amount of material, and it can be fascinating. I could never have imagined the role several of my paternal ancestors played in the development of the United States in the Colonial days. I had no clue.

My paternal ancestors came to the United States first from their country of origin, Firsby, Lincolnshire, England and later from Nova Scotia, Canada. They settled in the New England colonies of Massachusetts and Maine; later they branched out elsewhere. Some fought in the Civil War and the Revolutionary War. Since my reunion Memorial Day, Veteran's Day, and Independence Day have taken on new meanings for me, ones that are more personal.

In addition to my ancestors who were among the first settlers of Groton, Massachusetts, one young lady, captured by the Abenaki Indians and sold to the French in Montreal later became the first North American nun.

The difference in religion hasn't been an obstacle in reuniting with my paternal family. Those that have chosen not to accept me did it for personal reasons having nothing to do with this difference. It has just been harder for them to accept some facts of their past lives that they were never told about before. I can understand them as I appeared suddenly out of nowhere as if I was an alien who landed on their doorstep from a different planet, as far as they were concerned. Sometimes, it's just a matter of time; sometimes they'll never come to terms with it. That's life and I'm fine with that. I'm grateful for those who have accepted me into the family and with whom I maintain contact with so many years later.

18
Seven Years Later

In 2003 when mom heard I was scheduled for a complete hysterectomy on March 10th, she offered to come out to help. I gladly accepted, knowing how hard it would be for my husband to work and run the household. Besides, I would be alone all day, so I could use some help at that time. And it was a great opportunity to get to know each other even more. She arrived a few days before so we had some time to spend together before I was out of it for a while. We had been discussing the prospect of her adopting me back to make my status of daughter official, since we had no records to prove it.

All the records that possibly exist remain sealed in New York. To date, New York has still not opened records for access to adoptees. She brought it up again so I called around, found an attorney in Seattle who agreed to a reasonable price, and arrangements were made for her to meet with him. This meeting took place a few days after I returned home from the hospital. A date was set for the court appearance to finalize the adoption. Believe me, I was in so much pain and in no mood for this at all, but I knew that if it wasn't done at that time, it wouldn't get done. I took the pain in stride and accompanied by my mom, we set out for the courthouse. Here I was forty-seven years old and going through a second adoption. This one I would remember forever. What a feeling!

When my daughter married in March 2009, I invited my

mom to attend. She flew in from Toronto for the weekend, not an easy trip for a woman in her seventies, but one that was greatly appreciated as this was the first family celebration we were able to be together. I was elated. It was my dream coming true in the fullest sense of the word. The only thing that overshadowed my happiness that day was the arm pain I experienced at the time. It was later diagnosed as angina.

In 2007, my legs hurt so much from my lower back pain that I could not walk much. I saw several orthopedic surgeons all of whom claimed I wasn't a candidate for surgery, but none of them took an x-ray. I found out about one surgeon who specialized in a minimal invasion procedure and went to see him. The first thing he did was take an x-ray, and the evidence was there: I was definitely a surgical candidate. From the day of the surgery, that severe leg pain never surfaced again. The six weeks of recovery weren't the easiest, but they were worth it.

By July 2010, I had come a long way since that day in June 1996 and it's been an exciting and interesting journey. I've discovered that Mom and I share similar likes when it comes to Scrabble and Bingo; dogs; a country lifestyle; potato pancakes with applesauce, apples, chicken, and fish; reading autobiographies; doing jigsaw puzzles; Sunday as the favorite day of the week (is it because I was born on a Sunday?); and we both hate scrubbing the floor. With my half-sister Rachel our similar likes are the royal blue color; the spring; chocolate, blueberries, eggplant, chicken, and lamb; reading, though our choice of genres differs; the movie Mamma Mia; doing crossword puzzles; and a lucky number seven.

It is now 2012 and in August, I underwent a surgical procedure on my left lung for pleural effusion, a fancy term for liquid accumulation, and spent five days in the hospital. The medical issues never seem to stop, but life goes on.

Having made contact despite all odds, having searched and being found, having my birth mother adopt me back as an adult, and having my birth mother attend my daughter's wedding, were all unimaginable just over a decade ago. Now that they've all taken place, I am truly convinced that dreams can come true, but to make them do so requires persistence and passion to never give up. And now, September 2013, two months before my middle son, Shai, takes the next step in life when he marries Natalie, my mom will be there alongside the family to take part in this celebration.

Afterword

It's now April 2016. I've come a long way since that day in June 2006 and it's been an exciting and interesting journey. I continue learning about my heritage through genealogy research. There is so much to learn and parts of it are truly amazing.

To all my readers, both inside and outside of the adoption circle, I hope my story gives you a broader view of what it is like to be an adoptee, what it's like to wonder about the unknown, and what it's like to search and be found. I hope that after reading my memoir you will better understand those you know who are touched by adoption and the challenges that come along with it.

To all adoptees, birth parents, and adoptive parents involved in a search, my advice is that when you feel ready and can handle the stress and the outcome of your search, that is the time to be persistent in searching and never, ever, ever give up. No matter how much or how little information you have to go on, there's always some kind of light at the end of the tunnel. If I could do it with the little information I had, and that goes for my birth mother as well, anyone can. And don't forget that today you have the added resource of DNA testing that can help. I wish you all good luck in your searches and a wonderful ending to that empty black hole feeling.

General feedback is always welcome, so if this book in any

way inspires you to begin searching, to restart a search that has hit brick walls time and again, leading you to a successful reunion, or any other comment you wish to share I'd like to hear from you. E-mail me at gloria.oren@gmail.com.

Thank you for reading!

Dear reader,

I hope you enjoyed *Bonded at Birth: An Adoptee's Search for Her Roots*. I have to tell you, it has been quite therapeutic in writing my story.

As an author, I love feedback. Candidly, you're the reason I dug deep into my journey from adoption to reunion. So tell me what you liked, what you loved, even what you hated. I'd love to hear from you. You can write me at gloria.oren@gmail.com and visit me on the web at http://gloriaoren.com.

Finally, I need to ask a favor. If you're so inclined, I'd love a review of *Bonded at Birth*. Loved it, hated it — I'd just enjoy your feedback. Reviews can be tough to come by these days, and you, the reader, have the power to make or break a book. If you have time, here's a link to my author page, along with all my books on Amazon:

http://amazon.com/author/gloriaoren

Thank you so much for reading *Bonded at Birth* and for spending time with me.

In gratitude,

Gloria Oren

Gloria Oren

Appendix 1
Resources for Searching Online

You've decided to search, but don't know where to start. Let me tell you a secret: it doesn't matter where you start, as long as you keep moving forward. To get you started I provide the following suggestions for you to try as a leap into your journey of discovery.

Yahoo groups:

Adoption Reunion Registry

http://dir.groups.yahoo.com/group/Adoption-Reunion-Registry

Adoption Search Angels

http://dir.groups.yahoo.com/group/Adoption-Search-Angels

Adoption Search and Support

http://dir.groups.yahoo.com/group/AdoptionSearchandSupport

Soaring Angels

http://dir.groups.yahoo.com/group/SoaringAngels

theregistry

http://dir.groups.yahoo.com/group/theregistry

Search Tools:

Adoption Registry Connect

http://www.adopteeconnect.com/q/

Cyndi's List

http://www.cyndislist.com/adoption.htm

Yahoo! People Search

http://people.yahoo.com

Social Security Death Index

http://search.ancestry.com/search/db.aspx?dbid=3693

Adoption Search & Reunion

http://reunion.adoption.com/

Person Locator and Adoption-Related Links

http://www.daddezio.com/adoption

For Adopted Individuals

http://www.adopt.org/adopted-individuals

Adoption Database

http://www.adoptiondatabase.org/

G's Adoption Registry

http://www.gsadoptionregistry.com/

Email lists:

Uppity Adoptees

http://groups.yahoo.com/group/UppityAdoptees

Rootsweb's list of adoptee mailing lists

http://www.rootsweb.ancestry.com/~jfuller/gen_mail_adoption.
html?cj=;&o_xid=0001029688&o_lid=0001029688#1950_adoptees

Appendix 2
Family Surnames

Maternal Surnames

ALPERT

BEHRMAN

BERMAN

BOORD

BURGER

CALP

CLARKE

DEVENISHKIJ

DISTENFASS

FALLON

FRITZ

GIMEL

GOLDBERG

HAYTHORNWAITE

JONAS

KAYATSKY

LIFSHITZ

LOOMIS

NOVOPLYANSKIJ

ROSS

RUEFF

SCHARPE

SCHULMAN

SCHUSTER

STANLEY

TROSSMAN

VALENTINE

WHITE

Paternal Surnames

AETHELUWULF KING OF ENGLAND

AETHELRED PRINCESS OF ENGLAND

AINSWORTH

ALFRED THE GREAT KING OF ENGLAND

ALQIFU (AELFBED) QUEEN OF ENGLAND

ANDREWS

BAINES

BATE

BEAL (BEALE)

BEALES

BEALS

BRIDGET

BULCOKE

CHARLTON

COOMBS

CRISPE

CUTTER

DE BOLD

DE LA POOL

DE LONG (DELONG)

DE LUNGVILLERS

DE NEVILLE

DEWEY

DODGE

DRAPER

EALDGYTH PRINCESS OF NORTHUMBRIA

EALSWITH OF GAINAI

EARL OF NORTHUMBERLAND DUNBAR

ECKBERT III KING OF WESSEX

Paternal Surnames, continued

EDGAR "THE PEACEABLE" KING OF ENGLAND

EDMUND I "THE MAGNIFICENT" KING OF ENGLAND

ETHELRED "MUCIL" EAID OF THE GAINAI

FADBURN

FITZCRINNAN

GOFFE

HAYNESWORTH

LAMBERT

LOKER

REDBURH QUEEN OF WESSEX

PEARSON

PRESCOTT

SHARP

TOWER

WORTHYLAKE

EDWARD I (THE ELDER) KING OF ENGLAND

ELFRIDA (ELTHRYTH) QUEEN OF ENGLAND

ELQIFU PRINCESS OF ENGLAND

ETHELRED II "THE UNREADY" KING OF ENGLAND

ELQIVQ QUEEN OF ENGLAND

FAIRBANK

FIELD

FITZDOLPHIN

FITZMALDRED

GANNETT

GASPATRIC EARL OF NORTHUMBERLAND

GAWKROGER

Paternal Surnames, continued

GRISWALD

HARDIN

HARRINGTON

HILLIARD

HOBART

KENT

LANE

LAURILLIARD

LEATHERHEAD

LONGLEY

NEVILLE

PARKER

PALMER

PEASE

PLATTS

RADCLIFFE

RIPLEY

SABEAN

SAWTELL

SHADWIN

SHAW

STANDISH

STONE

THOMSON

UCHTRED OF NORTHUMBERLAND

UGHTRED EARL OF NORTHUMBRIA

WILKINS

Note: *Some names listed above still need document verification but have been listed by several people searching the same family info on genealogical sources.*

Made in the USA
Columbia, SC
11 December 2021

51023133R00098